ACKNOWLEDGEMENTS

All students of nonverbal communication owe a debt of gratitude to a handful of pioneering scientists. Chief among those is Charles Darwin, and more recently, Ray Birdwhistell, Albert Mehrabian, and Paul Ekman.

This book would not have been possible without the help of Fred Zimmerman and David Walbridge, who assisted with the writing, and William Pack, who assisted with the editing. Nor would it have been possible without Judy O'Brien, who insisted for over a decade that I should get busy writing.

Christopher Carter

Edited by Fred Zimmerman

Student

Body Language

Carter Entertainment

First publication 2014 by Christopher Carter

821 Winmoor Drive, Sleepy Hollow,Il, 60118

www.christophercartermentalist.com

ISBN# 978-0-9904078-0-5

Visit christophercartermentalist.com to read more about all of Christopher Carter's books and to buy them. You will also find news of Mr. Carter's events and you can sign up for e-newsletters so that you'll always be first to hear about any new releases.

DEDICATION

Dedicated to generations of mentalists who understood that observation was functionally indistinguishable from mindreading.

Dedicated also to all those who find human behavior endlessly fascinating.

TABLE OF CONTENTS

I. INTRODUCTION

WHAT IS BODY LANGUAGE? WHY SHOULD ANYONE STUDY IT?

You will spend your entire life learning to communicate orally, but the actual words you speak will be only part of the messages you communicate. Every day of your life, you send out hundreds of *nonverbal* messages; messages about who you are, what you want, and how you're feeling. And everything you **do**, from the way you stand, the gestures you use, and even the clothing you wear, sends messages to the outside world. The purpose of this book is to help you learn more about this "unspoken" language – both your own, as well as that of other people – and about adding new tools to your communication arsenal, with the ultimate goal of improving your college (and life) experience.

Hi, I'm Chris, or more formally, Christopher. You know … the guy who wrote this book. I'd like you to imagine that I'm sitting across from you, leaning back, and smiling. I'm wearing my standard work outfit: dress pants, sport coat, and tee-shirt. I'm also facing you with my hands open, with my palms up.

Why am I painting this word picture? Because I want you to like and trust me.

1

Even in this imaginary description, you react to what you "see," consciously and unconsciously. This, in a nutshell, is what this book is all about, nonverbal communication, or, to be exact, messages that are communicated without the use of words.

For students, nonverbal communication is very important because attending school is not just about learning … it's also about socializing—meeting people who may become a very important part of your life.

Let me be very clear; there is more to body language than gathering useful information by interpreting someone else's gestures or looks, it's also about the messages _you_ send.

Have you ever wondered how nonverbal information shapes your day-to-day interactions? You're about to find out.

In this book, I'll cover the basics of body language, with a special emphasis on the "student" experience. Sending the right message is important, not just for job interviews, but also during meetings with your Professors, on dates, and even in the simplest everyday interactions.

How this book is organized?

The first section of this book focuses on learning how to read people. These basic skills will help you understand how to spot nonverbal cues, and to understand what they mean. The second section is about applying your knowledge of body language to specific life situations, and about building your skill set.

Each chapter discusses a specific activity, e.g. dating, detecting lies, exhibiting leadership, etc. You may start reading from the beginning of the book, and continue in a linear fashion, or you may choose to jump from chapter to chapter, choosing the topics that most interest you. That's OK - each chapter stands alone.

I realize there is a LOT of information in this book, including stories, tips, and high-level scientific research. Don't worry, there won't be a quiz – life is hard enough! As you begin to read, you will immediately learn things that will change the way you communicate.

MY BACKGROUND

I've been a stage performer and professional speaker for most of my life, giving presentations at colleges and businesses all over the country. I make my living communicating with people, and one of the most fascinating things I continually encounter is how people say one thing *with their words*, while their *bodies* say something else entirely.

Body language is so common – and so misunderstood – that I was surprised to learn how few people study it. After all, you can't help but send nonverbal signals during every interaction you have …even online!

As a big believer in science, I've tried to document as much of the information contained in this book as I can, and at the same time, I've tried very hard to make this book relevant, useful, and readable. There are many notes at the back of the book as well to direct you to further study, and I'll continue adding interesting links on **christophercartermentalist.com** as I discover them.

HOW DID I GET HERE?

People are often amazed at how, with just one look, I can discern a variety of things about them: their favorite music, where they're from, and their major. It's not a trick - I will be the first to tell you that I don't read minds. What I *actually* do is ... I study people, and then I analyze what they are saying verbally and nonverbally. It's merely observation and science, and you can do it too.

Each of us is a product of millions of different experiences, and these experiences shape our goals, our values, and our sense of humor; essentially, they shape who we are. **But, by far, the most important of these experiences are those that involve other people.** True, some of us may read a book or see a movie that changes our lives, but I believe that if you were to pinpoint your *most* formative experiences, they will most likely involve direct, face-to-face communication with other people. There is no escaping the fact that **we are social creatures**.

Let me share with you two of my most important formative experiences. These are the encounters that led me to develop

my **Student Body Language** program, and ultimately, to write this book.

The first experience happened when I was around ten years old....

My parents bought me a Magic set. Women won't understand this, but men will testify that it is apparently a Federal Law in the United States that every boy around the age of ten must be given a Magic set. Most boys play with a few tricks, discover girls, and then throw the whole thing away. Not me ... I was hooked!

A strange thing happens when you put a Magic trick into the hands of a socially inept child. You wind up with one of the most irritating creatures known to man – the "pick-a-card kid." Everywhere my parents took me, I would be a half-step behind them asking anyone within earshot, "Let me show you a trick." After a few years of this, they huddled together and decided, "We *must* find this kid some other interests!"

One of their brilliant ideas was to ship me off to rural Arkansas for a few weeks in the summer to visit my Uncle Bud. Uncle Bud was a retired United States Army Colonel and an avid outdoorsman. The plan was for us to spend some time doing "guy things." In a way, we did. Every Wednesday night was poker night, and it was my privilege to stay up late and watch. Of course, I wasn't allowed to play; my job was ashtray-emptier and pretzel-fetcher. It didn't take me long to notice that, even though my Uncle loved the game of poker, he stunk at it! Whenever he had a decent hand, he would twist and fidget with his wedding band. I didn't know exactly what was going on, but I could definitely sense it was important. This, as you've already guessed, was one of the first times I started noticing "body language"... and its effects.

When I returned home at the end of the summer, I told my Mom what I had seen. My Mom - a licensed therapist with a background in psychology - told me that what I had seen was "body language." Ever helpful, she went to her bookshelves and pulled down a few volumes on the topic. She couldn't have known it at the time, but she was creating a monster. From that moment forward, *I became fascinated with the idea that people could telegraph their thoughts through their behavior*, and I realized I could use that fact to my advantage performing Magic.

Within a short time I had developed a routine in which I figured out which playing card a person is thinking of by merely asking questions, and watching their nonverbal reactions. When I performed this for people, their responses were beyond my wildest dreams. Instead of reacting with mere surprise, people were *astonished*. It wasn't uncommon to hear exclamations like, **"Oh my God, you're inside my head!"** When that happened, this socially-inept little boy knew exactly what he wanted to do when he grew up. I wanted to perform Magic - but not the traditional types of tricks commonly associated with Magicians, e.g. cut-and-restored ropes, illusions of all kinds, or knuckle-busting manipulations. I wanted to do Magic that floored people; Magic that happened - or appeared to happen - inside their heads. I had started on the road to becoming a professional Mentalist.

My second formative experience occurred more recently. I had completed a show at a small Liberal Arts college, and afterwards, as it often happens, the Campus Activities Committee took me out to dinner. They took me to Applebee's™.

It's always Applebee's™.

There were seven of us sitting around a large, high-top table. Since I'm always up-front about the psychological component of my show, I was being peppered with questions about body language, and about my "people reading" skills. In these circumstances, I'm repeatedly asked the same questions, such as, *"Is it true that if a person has her arms crossed, it means she's resistant to what you're saying?"* The answer, by the way, is no. It *can* mean that, but body language depends on context. It's equally possible that she's just cold (meaning her body temperature, not emotionally). Another common question is, *"Is it true that a person who's lying won't look you in the eyes?"* The answer is again, no. In fact, liars often exhibit very intense eye contact.

Then, **I was asked a question that changed my life**. A student sitting to my left - a young man named Michael - asked, *"How can I tell when a woman is interested in me?"*

I wanted very much to answer his question, but I couldn't.

Here's why:

There were six students sitting at the table, all of them looking directly at me. However, only five of them had their bodies oriented toward me. One, a girl sitting directly across the table from Michael, had her *face* turned toward me, but her *torso* faced Michael. Furthermore, whenever he would glance in her direction, she would tilt her head to the side, exposing the side of her neck to him. We typically only engage in this behavior when we feel affectionate or comfortable toward somebody. Even more significant, as he glanced at her, she would brush her hair back, exposing more of her face. Whenever he moved, she unconsciously mirrored his movements. If he leaned forward, she would too. If he reached out to pick up a utensil, so would she. In short, what she was demonstrating was classic, flirting body language.

Michael's question was, *"How can I tell when a woman is interested in me,"* and I couldn't answer without saying, "**Dude, wake up … she's right there!**"

That evening, when I returned to my hotel, I found myself wondering, *"What would Michael's life be like if he were able to read between the lines of human behavior?"* Clearly, his idea of a successful college experience included having a girlfriend, and participating in a romantic relationship. What if I could give him the skills to make that more likely?

That night, the idea for this book was born.

So now it's time for you to jump in and begin learning some of the most important skills you'll ever need during your college career, and, quite frankly, during the rest of your life.

Right now, I know what you're thinking …

WHY SHOULD I CARE ABOUT BODY LANGUAGE?

Reason One: 50 to 90% of all human communication is nonverbal.

Consider this: When you're listening to your Professor, friend, coach, etc., and you're only listening to their *words*, <u>you're failing to hear half of what is being said.</u> You're missing out on a world of meaning and nuance. And since the goal of business and social interactions is clear and concise communication, it is very important to accurately monitor the feedback from your listeners to ensure that you're being properly understood.

Reason Two: People will believe your *body* before they believe your *words*.

The majority of people have a limited understanding of what their body is saying, and many haven't a clue. So, if you're unaware of your own nonverbal cues, it's fairly certain you're "saying" things you don't intend.

Reason Three: Our brains interpret nonverbal signals on an unconscious or sub-conscious level.

Every moment that we're interacting with someone, our senses are taking in thousands of pieces of information, and our subconscious mind is using them to form opinions and make judgments. Of course, the other person is doing the same thing. But there's a problem: ***Our unconscious mind often gets it wrong.***

So, unless you become *consciously* aware of how your *unconscious* mind responds to nonverbal cues, you'll experience the same miscommunications over and over again.

WHAT IS BODY LANGUAGE?

The phrase "body language" represents all of the nonverbal behaviors that convey information to others. However, those behaviors are not limited to physical gestures and facial expressions, and many of them are unintentional. People send unintentional nonverbal signals all the time, in virtually every interaction, and they normally do it often unconsciously, revealing information they are trying to hide. (See the Chapter on "Lying" for more on this)

WHY STUDY BODY LANGUAGE?

Being able to read and understand people on a variety of levels increases confidence. Frankly, it's also a lot of fun to have a deeper understanding of what another person is thinking and feeling. Body language often accounts for a large percentage of our *total* communication, so without it, you're actually only getting half the story. Conversely, it's also important to understand what *you* are continually communicating to others nonverbally; remember, people react more to how we act than to what we say. Finally, this knowledge will give you a decided advantage in all facets of life, whether it's in a job hunt, a classroom interaction, or in the dating world.

HOW DOES BODY LANGUAGE WORK?

Some body language is intentional; the raised eyebrow, the sly grin, the smiling wave. Yet, a great deal of it is **un**intentional. Our bodies routinely reveal what we're thinking and feeling through unconscious actions and body positions. Much of this behavior goes unnoticed … by us. But it doesn't go unnoticed by others. They are taking in volumes about what you're *truly* thinking and feeling, if only on a subconscious level.

The goal of this book is to make you more aware of the messages you're sending, as well as those being sent to you.

HOW MUCH?

Most books that explore this topic eventually make the observation that nonverbal language accounts for up to 95% of all communication; 55 % from body language, 33 % from tone of voice, and the remaining 7 % from words. If you've run across this statement, you may have thought, "That can't be right." Well, it isn't. The 95% part has been shown to be fairly accurate, but the distribution is not.

This claim comes from a study implemented in the late 1960s by Albert Mehrabian. In it, he references an experiment in which a select group of college students were read a number of emotionally charged words, with the speaker using a variety of tones-of-voice and inflections. Afterwards, these students were asked what they felt the speaker meant by each word. Mehrabian concluded that whenever there was a difference of opinion between the "dictionary" meaning of a word, and the "perceived" meaning of a word, that difference was due to the speaker's nonverbal cues.

In other words, when two people communicate, HOW a person says something takes precedence over WHAT is being said. Mehrabian then created the 55%/33%/7% distribution. But this distribution is not that cut-and-dried.

While it is clear that HOW we say something affects WHAT is understood, there's more to it than that. The emotional content and intention in our messages is also a big factor. For example, when trying to teach the workings of a particular economic theory, nonverbal cues will most likely play only a small part. However, when trying to persuade someone to follow a particular school of economic thought, nonverbal cues may loom large. The reason for this is plain—people are not normally persuaded through reason alone. Factors such as emotion, empathy, trust, and credibility play a crucial role, and this type of information is normally communicated nonverbally. It's also important to note that even when trying to teach something dry and technical, negative nonverbal cues can undermine the effort.

A more accurate way to summarize the current research is, "***Depending on circumstances*, nonverbal cues can account for between 50 to 80% of what we communicate.**" The key here is the phrase, "*depending on circumstances*," because the emotional content of the message greatly affects how we perceive it.

There is, however, one circumstance that practically never changes; selling yourself. Even if you are not a professional salesperson, you're always selling your ideas, your integrity, your personality, and your trustworthiness. This kind of information is conveyed almost exclusively through nonverbal channels. This is why you must be aware of your own body language 100% of the time.

BODY LANGUAGE AT SCHOOL

College life is filled with situations where communication is primarily nonverbal: the classroom, student clubs, the cafeteria, student/teacher interactions, and, of course, campus social life. (This list is not exhaustive.) If you are to succeed in each of these arenas, you must be able to sense and interpret the complex network of social cues others emit, as well as your own. Without this dual awareness, you will not have the advantage of better understanding others, and you will almost certainly radiate messages you don't intend.

What if you could learn how to sit with a friend who is undergoing a personal crisis and "read between the lines" to better understand what he or she may not be telling you?

What if you could sit in a classroom and deduce from your professor's behavior the material that is most likely to be included on the next quiz or exam?

14

What if you could learn how to carry yourself in such a way that your Professors will not only wish to give you extra help and attention, but it may cause them to give you a better grade?

Wouldn't any of these skills be useful to you?

Developing them, and more, is the goal of this book.

If you take away nothing else, take away this: human communication is goal-oriented. We communicate in order to get results. Therefore …

… the better you communicate, the more successful you will be.

Let's begin.

The "WHAT" of Body Language

II. WHY CAN WE READ BODY LANGUAGE?

Reading body language is not always complicated. In fact, you've been doing it all of your life.

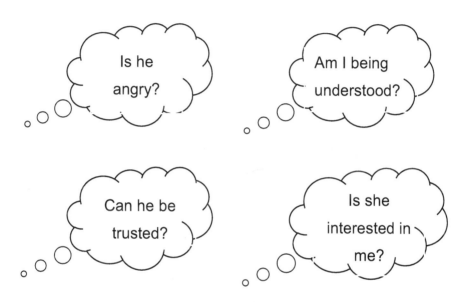

While we may not *consciously* notice every nonverbal cue we see, we always react *unconsciously,* and both of these reactions cause noticeable physical reactions. This is what we will explore in this chapter—how different parts of the brain interact, and how our conscious and unconscious thoughts result in noticeable, readable "body language,"

Before we begin discussing brain physiology, here's a fun experiment that will provide a quick peek into how the brain works. You can do this yourself, but it may work better if you lead someone else through it:

1.   Have a friend clasp their hands together with their fingers intertwined, and hold their clasped hands up in front of their face.

2.   Tell them to extend their index fingers like a steeple, and then to separate the tips of their fingers about two inches or so. Their palms should be pressed tightly together.

3.   Ask your friend to stare at the point directly in between the tips of the fingers, and to not take their eyes off that point.

While they're doing this, say the following:

"Stare directly at the space between the tips of your fingers and visualize what I'm saying. Imagine I'm wrapping the tips of your fingers with a big, fat, red rubber band ... see that red rubber band wound tightly around the tips of your index fingers ... and see that big, fat, red rubber band start to pull the tips of your fingers closer and closer together. As the tips of your fingers start to move, just go with it. Let it happen. Watch that red rubber band as it pulls tighter and tighter, closer and closer, until the fingers start to touch ..."

You may need to repeat certain phrases over and over, but you will find that, after a while, the person's fingers will start to move. At first, the movement may be slight, and they may try to resist. If that happens, remind them to not actively fight it, but to relax and let it happen. Invariably, their fingers will start to move together.

> *When I do this in my lectures, the audience typically breaks out into self-conscious laughter as they realize the movement is happening apparently on its own. They truly feel as if "they" have nothing to do with it.*

If you tried this on yourself and it worked, congratulations! You are a hypnotist's dream; you are highly suggestible. You are not alone—everybody responds to suggestion, at least a bit. In fact, the only way to perform this exercise and *not* have your fingers come together is to deliberately work against it …and even then, you are responding, if only in a negative way.

In reality, of course, your mind has everything to do with it. Your fingers move as a result of something called the **Ideomotor Response**. Put simply, when you hear how your fingers *ought* to move, your subconscious mind_*tells* them to move. Your conscious mind may want to change this behavior—and often does—but the point here is that two parts of your brain are working both separately, and together.

This demonstration illustrates an important point; all of our physical movements originate in the mind; some consciously, others unconsciously. We are often not aware of the actions created by our unconscious mind. If we want to throw a ball, our brain sends a series of impulses to our arms and shoulders, and the ball is thrown. We are conscious of this – we've made a conscious choice to throw the ball. However, many of our actions are produced *unconsciously*. Setting aside bodily functions e.g. breathing, the heart beating, and other bodily functions that are hard-wired into our brain stem, our subconscious mind is always working, and is always producing physical actions.

This is very important to understand in the study of body language. Once you understand where body language originates (in the brain), the different ways it is created (consciously vs. unconsciously), and how it manifests itself physically (deliberately or instinctively), you will be better able to notice it, and understand it.

TWO BRAINS

Imagine you are looking at a photograph of a man who appears enraged. His muscles are tensed, his hand is closed into a fist, and his arm is cocked. You know instantly what this man feels, and you can pretty accurately predict what he's about to do. This analysis happens instantly, without you having to "think" about it.

Something else is happening as well. When you see this picture, your blood pressure increases, and blood starts flowing to your muscles in preparation to either fight or flee. Now, since the stimulus is only a photo, this response may be weak, but the difference between a real or imagined threat is measured in degrees, not in kind. Either way, your body reacts.

So what's happening? It's only a picture, after all. But your unconscious brain doesn't know that. Your eyes send the information gleaned from the picture to the part of your brain called the *cognitive unconscious*, located mid-brain in the region called the amygdala. The chief function of the amygdala is comparing new information to information stored in memory, then predicting what will happen next. Once it has made its prediction, it tells the rest of your body how to react, whether you like it or not. Without your conscious consent, your cognitive unconscious prepares your body to fight or flee.

The amygdala does this in the time it took to read the first word in this sentence.

This part of your mind is called the cognitive *unconscious* to distinguish it from your *conscious* mind. Our conscious minds are self-aware and analyze information in a linear fashion. Our *unconscious* minds are not self-aware, and process information … well … unconsciously. It can't always be controlled and it can't be shut off.

> *I call the cognitive* **unconscious** *your* **Caveman Brain,** *and the cognitive* **conscious** *your* **Modern brain.**

All mammals have a caveman brain. It evolved to initiate quick responses to a world filled with potential threats. Our species would not have survived if we weren't able to instinctively defend ourselves, sense danger, or run away from a threat. It also influences our emotions by creating powerful desires for things it thinks will keep us alive and healthy, as well as powerful aversions to things it thinks will harm us. Most importantly, we are not always aware of what the caveman brain is thinking or doing. The caveman brain's actions are not thoughtful … they are instinctive. This means that it is difficult for the caveman brain to distinguish between real threats and imagined ones.

Consider the photo again: your caveman brain created the fight or flight response unconsciously, but your *modern* brain—larger in mammals and located in the cerebral cortex so it can control your higher reasoning functions—analyzed that response, and decided the threat wasn't real. After the initial fear response, your breathing began to slow, your muscles relaxed, and you stayed calm.

Note the sequence of events:

•   The caveman brain created the emotional and physical response instinctively (unconsciously).
•   The modern brain *consciously* reviewed that response.
•   The modern brain decided the response was inappropriate, and changed it.

Why is this process so important to note? First, it illustrates that our modern brain and caveman brain are often at odds with one another. Second, while in this instance the modern brain was able to adjust the reaction, this isn't always the case. Furthermore, the modern brain is not always aware of what the caveman brain is up to.

Why? Because nature has given the modern brain only a tiny fraction of the processing power it gave to the caveman brain, which often leads to the modern brain being overwhelmed by the behaviors created by the caveman brain. When caveman behavior bypasses the modern brain, *voila*, body language is born.

However, the astute observer will notice how the photo caused you to react unconsciously, and that the reaction was then controlled consciously. To recognize unconscious responses and control them consciously is what this book will teach you to do.

To be sure, this "two brain" analysis is oversimplified, but it is important to understand that body language originates in the mind, both consciously and unconsciously, and it's up to us to notice the physical reactions these thoughts are creating.

> *I often tell people that they're already good at reading body language ...*
> *... they just don't know it yet.*

Even though some body language is very easy to notice and understand, the majority of it is often *not so easy* to read.

People are well practiced at masking their true feelings. For example, if you're on a job interview, you will normally try to appear confident, and you'll probably do a pretty good job of it, even though you're very nervous. If you're at a party and stuck in a conversation with someone you dislike, your up-bringing has taught you how to appear as if you're having a great time to appease social norms, and the people around you will probably believe that you are. But in both situations, your modern brain may be overwhelmed with caveman stimulus, and you are probably sending out lots of nonverbal cues that reveal your true feelings.

Bottom line: Human beings are dishonest.

This isn't necessarily a bad thing. Human beings couldn't function if we continually expressed our true feelings. Consciously monitoring and shaping our social interactions is a fundamental part of living in a society. Because we know this, we also know that it would be extremely useful to penetrate these appearances to learn what's truly going on underneath.

So what do we call this information that evades the modern brain? Time to learn a new word:

> Leakage: *noun* \ˈlē-kij\: an occurrence in which secret
> information becomes known.

"Leakage" is an unfortunate term that describes the moments when behavior instigated from the caveman brain "leaks" past our modern brain, revealing what a person is truly feeling.

For our purposes, "leakage" is our best friend.

During my lectures, I often bring a man and woman onstage for a role-playing game. I have them sit in chairs facing one another, and I tell them to imagine that they're on a date, and the romantic chemistry is perfect. Then I ask, "What is you caveman brain telling your body to do?" I also ask them to keep it clean.

They normally say, "The caveman brain is telling us to kiss." or, "It's telling us to hold hands."

*What the two helpers seldom notice, however, is that <u>they've already started to align their chairs and bodies so that they're facing more directly toward each other,</u> and they've already started to scoot their chairs a bit closer together. **Just by imagining the scene, their caveman brains are already starting to prepare them for a romantic encounter!** And of course, the entire audience notices this right away.*

> *At this point, I stress the fact that public displays of affection could be socially inappropriate, so the modern brain wants them to look like proper ladies and gentlemen. In response, they shift back in their seats a little and pull their hands into their laps; however, their feet start to move a little closer. Their caveman brains are <u>still</u> at work, revealing their true feelings. Behavior has "leaked," and while the audience witnessed it, the participants are often unaware of it.*
>
> *But the real fun comes when I reverse the scenario. I tell them to imagine that they are on the same date, but this time it's going horribly. They can't stand each other. Immediately they start to lean back and close their bodies off to each other. It's not uncommon for them to cross their legs and arms, and they almost always angle their chairs away from each other. In the real life version of the scene, they may be stuck there for a while, each trying to act like he or she is having fun, but the truth always **leaks** out somewhere.*

PAYING ATTENTION

So how can you start noticing and evaluating another person's leakage?

A large part of interpreting body language is learning to pay attention. This means watching, listening, and actively observing behavior in a different way than you have been. We have become so used to doing the same things over and over, that we no longer react to, or even see, much of what occurs around us. We get up at the same time, eat the same food, go the same places, and see mostly the same group of people, so there's not much incentive to truly pay attention. One of the first skills you must embrace is noticing the people around you.

This is where you get to play Sherlock Holmes!

• **Observe people in a public area.** Notice their body language and, using your own experience as a guide, start to draw conclusions about what they're feeling. Start simply—that guy is in a hurry, that woman is carrying too much stuff. Then, transition to more detailed observations—is that person smiling because they know a secret, or because they just ate a cupcake?

• **Observe people in your classroom or lecture hall.** Notice your teacher's behavior and the students' reactions. Notice your OWN body language as well. How do their postures and attention spans shift when the material changes? Who is more interested? Who isn't? Who is interested in other students? Pay special attention when a substitute teacher or guest speaker attends class—how does everyone's behavior change? How does YOUR behavior change?

- **Observe your friends in social situations**. Take note of their "normal" behavior, and then notice when it changes, and try to discover why. Keep in mind that friends tend to mirror each other's behavior, so notice when that happens.

All of this will be new to you, so make it easy on yourself and let your subconscious mind be your guide; note how you're *feeling*, rather than what you're *thinking*. Does this place feel safe to me? Do I feel this person is truthful? Do I feel I'm being understood? These are good questions to keep in mind.

In order to be successful, you must believe in yourself and trust your instincts. We are emotional creatures, and our feelings have evolved to protect and teach us. Believe what they tell you, and you'll be on the road to becoming a great reader of body language.

Now that we've explored a general overview of body language, it's time to start discussing some specific tools and procedures that you will use for the rest of your life.

I call these…

III. THE BIG FOUR

Now that you 1) know where body language comes from, 2) know that it's possible to notice and interpret it, and 3) are now "paying attention" in a more focused way, you may be wondering what the physical cues you're noticing actually mean.

The first challenge you'll face is that the number of nonverbal behaviors you can observe is almost infinite. Consider facial expressions, Dr. Paul Ekman—a respected American psychologist who was a pioneer in the study of emotions and their relation to facial expressions—defined six core facial expressions that transcend cultures. I will be providing a brief overview of these later in this chapter, but since these six expressions can be combined into thousands of permutations, truly mastering them would take a great deal of intensive training.

> *Dr. Ekman has a training program available through his website, and I highly recommend it.*

Therefore, in this book we'll be taking a path toward a more obtainable goal. What follows is a list of four basic types of body language with which you should start. These four have been assembled specifically because they are "macro" behaviors; they are large and easy to spot once you know what you're looking for. At the same time, these behaviors provide an exceptionally large pool of clues about what a person is thinking and feeling from moment to moment, using the least amount of effort.

Let's call these: **The Big Four**, and for ease of memory, remember the acronym POPO:

- **P**roximity
- **O**rientation
- **P**acifiers
- **O**pen (or Closed) Body Language

If you train yourself to become aware of these basic clues—and nothing else—you will never look at people in the same way again.

Now, before we start exploring these behaviors, let's briefly review the types of nonverbal information they can reveal:

1) The nature of a person's relationships with other people:

- Who is dominant in a group? Who is less significant?
- Whom do specific people admire? Who admires them back?
- Who controls whom?

2) Where is a person's *real* interest at any given moment?

3) A person's attitudes toward others and about specific situations, e.g. whom do they like or dislike.

So let's dive into **The Big Four.**

I. PROXIMITY

Proxemics is the study of how we use the physical space around us. The first rule of it is:

• We tend to move closer to things we like or are interested in, and we tend to move farther away from things we dislike or are not interested in.

You may think this sounds obvious, but unless you actively note this behavior, and watch its progression, it could fly right past you. Imagine that you're at a party and somebody famous walks in. Even if you were the only person in the room who didn't know who that celebrity was, you would still be able to tell he or she was important merely by the way everyone gravitates toward them. It would be as if that person generated a magnetic field that drew people to them.

On the other hand, if at that same party, a guest arrived whom nobody liked, you would notice the way everyone moved away, almost as if they were repelled by reverse polarity.

Interestingly, the simple rule just described applies to "ideas" in the same way it does for people.

As a speaker, I can easily tell when people are interested in what I have to say by the way they lean toward me during a lecture. The reverse is also true. If I say something with which they disagree, they tend to lean their bodies away.

Not long ago, I was at a restaurant eavesdropping on the couple sitting across from me. It's what I do. From what I could gather, they were on a first date. As they conversed, she started to lean her body in towards his. Clearly, I noted, the woman was interested in the man. The conversation eventually switched to politics. The man mentioned the candidate he was supporting, and immediately the woman shifted back into a full, upright position. The poor guy didn't know it, but their political differences would be a big issue in whatever future relationship developed. If he had noticed her body language, he might have found a way to undo the damage to her perception of him. At the very least, he could have learned a valuable lesson about what not to discuss on a first date.

Please don't be tempted to think that just because a person has drawn very close to you that they think you're hot stuff. Spatial norms can vary tremendously from culture to culture, and even from person to person.

A BRIEF HISTORY OF SPATIAL NORMS

In the United States, we tend to maintain a relatively large circle of "personal space" around ourselves. When somebody enters that space without our permission, we can become agitated, even angry. But this isn't true everywhere.

In the United States, spatial norms change from region to region. In the Midwest, people tend to maintain a larger distance from each other, but on the West Coast, people are much more comfortable communicating closer together. Europe also experiences the same diversity, and in the Middle East, the space normally maintained between people gets smaller still. If you drill down into specific cultures around the globe, you will find people who are extremely protective of their personal space, as well as groups who don't seem to care at all. Therefore, how a person uses their personal space must be judged in the *context* of that person's culture, and the *context* of their own personal communication style.

The next time you're in a group that is dominated by a distinctly powerful personality, *pay special attention to the way that person occupies the space around them.* You'll find that they use a lot more of it than do the submissive members of the group. (Their stance may be a little wider, their gestures bigger, and their voice may be louder.) Continue paying attention and you'll find that the leader of the group is more likely to break into or violate the personal space of the underlings, while the underlings are more respectful and less likely to break into the personal space of the group leader.

Personal space is one way we define who has higher and lower status in society. In general, the higher your status, the more space you are afforded. There is no more glaring example of this than the difference between First Class and Economy on an airplane. The high status people are allowed to sit in large chairs with plenty of room, while the lower status people are crowded into the back.

II. ORIENTATION

Orientation refers to the direction we point our bodies. The rule here is that people tend to orient toward things they like or are interested in, and away from things they don't like or don't find interesting.

You may notice the use of the phrase 'orient toward' rather than 'face toward.' This is because the direction a person turns their head is often a less reliable indicator of where their interest or focus really lies. A more reliable indicator is where they orient the rest of their body.

In the previous chapter, we discussed how the "modern brain" is constantly monitoring our behavior and trying to control it in order to create the right kind of impression, and how it isn't always successful. This is one of those cases; the modern brain does a better job of controlling certain regions of our bodies than others. In particular, it does a better job of controlling the nonverbal behavior of our face and head, probably because we are acutely aware that other people gather a great deal of information from our facial expressions and eye contact.

However, the modern brain is less effective at controlling the behavior of our hands and arms, even less effective at controlling the behavior of our hips and torso, and least effective at controlling the behavior of our legs and feet. As a result, the best source of "leakage" is the lower parts of our bodies (those parts we are less consciously aware of, and therefore less able to control).

In fact, former FBI Special Investigator Joe Navarro calls the feet "the most honest parts of the body."

You can tell when a person with whom you're talking is truly giving you their undivided attention because their entire body—legs, torso, and feet—will be oriented toward you. If their mind is elsewhere, or they just want to make it seem as if they are paying attention to you, you will find the lower parts of their body oriented away from you and, perhaps, toward the true object of their interest.

Unlike Joe Navarro, who finds the direction of the feet most revealing, I find I get the most honest "tell" from the orientation of a person's hips. I can recall a striking example of this from a few years ago. It was after a college performance and a Student Activities Advisor had taken me to a bar (not Applebees!). We were sitting at a table having a pleasant conversation when she pointed to a man and woman standing at the bar and challenged me to read them.

After a few moments of observation, I noticed that, even though the woman was facing toward the man and smiling, her torso was angled significantly away from him. Although she was in conversation with him, she had opened up her body to the rest of the room. It was clear that she was anticipating the arrival of someone else.

I told my friend that the woman and man were not romantically involved, but they clearly knew and like each other, and that soon, her boyfriend would arrive and join the group. I also guessed, based on the woman's obvious comfort around the man, that her boyfriend would know him and that he would not be threatened by the other man's presence. Sure enough, after a short while, a man emerged from the bathroom and came up to her. He put his arm around her and kissed her on the lips. It was then that I could see the resemblance between the two men and realized that they were brothers.

III. PACIFIERS

Joe Navarro provided a name for what is considered to be one of the most useful concepts in body language: *Pacifier.* He uses this term to classify the behaviors we use to calm ourselves or soothe our minds.

For years, researchers have known that as our level of stress increases, so does our use of self-touch gestures. These gestures can take many forms and can be very idiosyncratic. For example, a man with a beard or mustache my stroke it; a woman with long hair may twirl it with her fingers. If a person is particularly stressed, he or she may pull at their collar, bite their own lip, or drum their fingers on the table.

Mr. Navarro's insight is that the function of these gestures is self-pacification. Whenever our anxiety level gets too high, we need a safety valve, and we turn to any of a thousand learned behaviors that help calm ourselves down.

Pacifying behaviors do not necessarily have to involve self-touch. They may also involve the manipulation of objects; chewing on a pen or on the end of a pair of eyeglasses are common pacifiers. Smoking and chewing gum are also common.

> *In my lectures, I list a handful of the more obvious pacifiers, and then open the floor to suggestions from the audience. Each time I do this, I always learn a few more that I hadn't considered. Recent examples include sitting on the hands, sucking the cheeks, and plucking nose hairs. Ouch!*

When you see a pacifier kick in, you are seeing evidence that that person's level of tension has risen.

What you can't know, at this point, is whether the increase in tension is due to something positive or negative. A person may start to use pacifiers when stressed by fear or anxiety, or, conversely, when excited and happy. What you need to do is look for other body language cues – or other external clues - that may reveal the source of the tension. *The important thing to remember is that people display pacifiers when they feel stress (good or bad), and when you see them, you should start looking for other cues that will help identify the cause.*

IV. OPEN BODY LANGUAGE.

If I tell you that somebody's body language is 'closed,' what would you imagine that looks like? You may have an image of a person with their arms or legs crossed, or their head pointing down. And you would be exactly right. Open body language, as you would expect, is the exact opposite: arms uncrossed, head up, torso exposed and unprotected. Open to the world.

In general, we tend to close our bodies off from those things we dislike or find threatening or unpleasant, and open our bodies up to things we like, trust, or find appealing.

> *I remember the first paid performance I ever did on a college campus. The student who was going to introduce me was a very outgoing and confident guy, right up to the point where he walked out onto the stage. The instant he got in front of the audience, he changed. He immediately shoved his hands down into his pockets, turned his head toward the floor, and brought his knees closer together. Psychologically, there was no difference for him between the audience's judgment of him, and the fear that the audience might physically attack him. The caveman brain sent signals to the muscles telling them to close in, protect the body, and make himself as small a target as possible.*

Here's the interesting point; it makes perfect sense that we close our body off to protect our physical being from something we perceive as a threat. But, <u>we use the same behavior to protect ourselves from psychological threats as well</u>. This is vital, and is a fact that we will explore in upcoming chapters.

MICRO-EXPRESSIONS

Clearly, familiarizing yourself with **The Big Four** will put you on a clear path to noticing and analyzing nonverbal cues. It's also important to understand that **The Big Four** is not, by any means, an exhaustive list. There is a WORLD of research out there that continues to delve deeper and deeper – and in greater detail – into the realm of nonverbal cues.

A pioneer of this research was Dr. Paul Ekman. In response to his mother developing mental illness, and eventually committing suicide, Dr. Ekman dedicated his life to the study of psycho-therapy, and helping people with mental disorders. One of the byproducts of his research was his work in defining systematic ways to *quantify* body language, including the cataloguing of our subtle facial expressions and their meanings.

Through research and experimentation, Dr. Ekman was able to determine that the small, almost undetectable facial expressions we make when interacting with others (which he labeled micro-expressions), and that were once thought to be specific to each culture across the globe, were, in reality, virtually universal. Further, if you became adept at identifying them, you could gain valuable insights into how a person was feeling at any given moment. This was seminal work, and the psychological community owes Dr. Ekman a great debt.

He defined a set of six universal facial expressions that we will review briefly here. In the 1990s, Dr. Ekman expanded this list to include many more subtle expressions, with more nuanced meanings, but for our purposes, learning about the basic six will be sufficient. They are:

Expression	Motion Cues
Happiness	Raising and lowering of mouth corners
Sadness	Lowering of mouth corners & raise inner portion of brows
Surprise	Brows arch / eyes open wide to expose more white / jaw drops slightly
Fear	Brows raised / eyes open / mouth slightly open
Disgust	Upper lip raised / nose bridge is wrinkled / cheeks raised
Anger	Brows lowered / lips pressed firmly together / eyes bulging

Remember, these are MICRO-expressions. By their written definition, they may sound a bit comical or cartoonish. if a person were to stand in front of you with their mouth agape, and their eyes bulging from their head, you'd probablysay there's nothing subtle going on here, and clearly, they are reacting to some imminent threat, such as a Kodiak Bear rounding the corner on its hind legs.

What Dr. Ekman observed were that humans, while interacting with other people, or even reading or thinking about a topic, emit small, almost imperceptible versions of the facial expressions described in this table. Furthermore, the "emitter" is rarely aware that they are doing so. This gives the trained observer a decided advantage when it comes to understanding what a person is thinking and feeling at a given time.

Entire books and college majors have been created to study this type of behavior, and I will be releasing a book in the future that adds my research on the topic, but for now, I include them here for the sake of completeness.

If you wish to explore these further, you may wish to visit www.paulekman.com where you'll be able to learn more about them, and actually take some visual tests to test your ability to identify them. It's fun, and you should give it a try.

THE WHOLE IS GREATER ....

Now that you are familiar with **The Big Four** – with a passing familiarity to the **6 Basic Ekman Facial Cues** - and are starting to "pay attention" to these behaviors in other people, it's important that you realize something important ... **if you notice one or more of these behaviors, you cannot immediately start making conclusions about what someone is thinking or feeling.** That is too easy. For example: if you're talking with someone, and that person crosses their arms, you may be tempted to quickly deduce that they are resistant to what you have to say. After all, crossed arms are the classic example of closed body language, right?

No, this isn't necessarily true. One piece of body language isn't significant by itself. Therefore, if a person's arms are crossed *(Open/Closed),* and you suspect they may not trust you, you should look for other signs to support your hypothesis. He may pull away from you *(Proximity)*, change his orientation *(Orientation)*, start a nervous habit *(Pacifiers)*, or some combination of all four. Then you can start drawing some tentative conclusions. At the very least, this observed behavior could inform how you choose your words, how you hold *your* body, and which conversational approaches to take (or not take).

These combinations may be misleading. Physical behavior *alone* cannot tell you precisely what that person is thinking or feeling—that can only be determined through *context* (there's that word again). This is what we will explore in the next chapter.

IV. ESTABLISHING A BASELINE

Once you start to pay attention to **The Big Four**, you will find you have a heightened level of awareness and sensitivity, as well as a clearer understanding of what people may be thinking and feeling. However, you will still be a long way from being an expert people-reader.

Up to this point, I have stressed the importance of context, and how "body language" cannot be evaluated in a vacuum; it must *always* be interpreted by taking into account the circumstances framing it. Here's an example:

Try this experiment with your friends. Tell them that you are going to play a game with them in which they play the role of liar and you play the role of truth detector. During the game, like a police interrogator, you'll be asking them questions and trying to determine when they're telling the truth, and when they are lying.

Here are the instructions:

1.   Explain to your friend that you are going to ask them three questions.

2.   Also explain that they should lie when answering one of the questions, and they should answer truthfully when answering the other two.

3.   Stress that they may choose ANY question to lie about—the first, second, or third—and they are not to reveal to you at any time which is which.

4.   Offer to help by saying that you will share all of the questions up front, and that they should decide FIRST which question to which they will lie, and then they should decide what *all* of their answers will be. This will help them maintain as much control over their physical reactions as possible.

The questions you ask should be ones they can easily answer, but they should also be questions to which you do not know the answers. For example:

- What is your mother's maiden name?
- What did you have for breakfast?
- In what city were you born?

You should be very clear about these instructions because in my experience, I have found that many of my helpers get so wrapped up in the game that they forget to lie and answer each question with the truth.

Responding to these questions with the truth will take no cognitive effort—the answers should be at their fingertips. On the other hand, responding with a lie will take a little mental work. Granted, not a lot, but significantly more than answering with the truth.

If you were asked what you had for breakfast, and told you should lie about it, you're going to spend a little effort searching your memory for an answer that is 1) not true, and 2) sounds plausible. This cognitive effort will show up in your helper's body language.

Here's the secret: as they give their answers, watch their eyes. You will observe that two out of three times they will move in one particular direction when they answer, while one time, their eyes will move in another direction. *That inconsistent movement is the body language that marks the lie!*

You will have a lot of fun trying this out, and in time, you may get quite a reputation for being an expert interrogator. In reality, it is ridiculously easy. But, other than having fun, what is the point of this game?

Have you ever heard that when somebody lies they look up and to the right, or up and to the left? Well, this isn't true. What is true, however, is that when a person engages in a cognitively challenging task, his eyes will move. In spite of what you may have read in other books about body language, there is no fixed relationship between the *direction* of eye movement and the nature of the cognitive effort. Some people, when thinking of a visual image, will look up, some will look down. Some people when thinking of a stored memory will look to the right. Some will look left.

49

With respect to our particular game, about half of the liars will look right, and half will look left. The key is that, in every case, they will look *in a different direction when lying than they will when telling the truth.*

If body language can only be understood in context, *then the most important context is how that person behaves most of the time.* If you notice that a person is using pacifiers, that observation means little if that person is a bundle of nerves all of the time. However, if that person is normally calm and collected, and *then* they begin to use pacifiers, you now have useful information. Additionally, if a person comes from a culture where personal space zones are very small, it tells you nothing if that person is intruding on your personal space. But if that person shares your origins (where personal space is larger), and *then* this person suddenly gets closer to you, or suddenly draws away from you, then you know that their mental or emotional state has changed, and you need to find out what is causing this change.

Trained interrogators recognize the importance of establishing a baseline for a person's behavior. It is, in my opinion, the single most important step in learning to read body language. Until you've established a baseline, you have almost no information from which to draw conclusions.

There is an added benefit to establishing a person's baseline behavior: it forces us to pay closer attention to the people with whom we communicate. Strange as it may sound, the main reason most of us have difficulty reading body language is that we have never taught ourselves to truly observe and pay attention to other people. We are far too busy thinking of ourselves.

THE FULL BODY SCAN

In the following sections, I'm going to share with you two techniques I use all the time to establish a baseline for other peoples' body language. I strongly recommend that you practice these techniques until they become habits. As you do, you will discover yourself noticing and acting upon a level of detail that you never thought possible.

Think of somebody with whom you spoke today. Can you remember what they were wearing? Were their clothes current, or out-of-date? How about their shoes? How was their hair cut? Were their nails long or short? What color were their eyes?

If you're like most people, you probably can't answer these questions, and there's a simple explanation why: you didn't take the time to look.

Several years ago, I had dinner with a Student Activities Advisor in Texas. I had just finished a series of performances for his school's summer orientation session, and we celebrated by going to a local steak house. During our conversation, he told me stories about his hard childhood—growing up in a gang-infested neighborhood in Houston. He had managed to break away from the gangs by turning to competitive martial arts. He also told me that his time in the gangs taught him to be particularly observant of his surroundings.

Whenever he was in a building, he said, he noted where the exits were, and precisely who was sitting where. He did this, he said, without ever consciously trying to. It had become such a part of his routine that he did it without thinking.

I'm pretty observant myself, and I never noticed him taking any extra stock of our surroundings. If he did do, as he claimed, he had so integrated the process into his regular social behavior that he did it unnoticeably. I decided to put him to the test. I asked him to describe the room we were in.

Without hesitation, he told me exactly where the exits were and gave what appeared to be accurate estimates of how far we were to each of them. He told me there were nine

> *guests at the tables, a bartender, a waitress, and a manager. I counted the people in the room. He was right. Then without ever taking his eyes off me, he proceeded to give a basic description of each of the guests and tell me which exit he or she was facing. I was impressed.*
>
> *I'll be honest with you. I make a living by observing details that most people overlook, and even I'm not as good as my friend. In fact, I'm not even close. But his was a habit born of necessity. Unless your life depends upon it, you or I may never become that observant.*
>
> *However, we can improve.*

The first step involves turning the act of observation into a ritual that we perform each time we encounter someone; a ritual that we perform as automatically as washing our hands before dinner.

Most of our conversations with people take place at what is called *social distance*. Typically, we will be standing between three and six feet from our conversation partner. Once we've begun talking, we're pretty much obligated to maintain eye contact. If we were to give the other person a "once over" at this point in order to catalogue the details of their personal appearance and body language, they would notice it immediately. Things would get … awkward.

The solution is to begin the process of scrutinizing nonverbal clues well before we get to the point of conversation. Get into the habit of scanning a person's body, noting every detail you can. Don't wait to start observing until you begin talking to them – start when they are at a distance. By the time you greet each other, shake hands, and begin your interaction, you've already begun to analyze their body language.

Your natural inclination will be to scan a person's body from head to toe. Try reversing the order: scan from their feet to their head. At first, this will feel uncomfortable. After all, we're naturally drawn toward faces, and naturally predisposed to make eye contact.

There are two reasons to scan from the feet upward:

• Precisely because we are naturally attracted to faces, you may tend to lock in on their facial expressions, and you will miss the many clues found in the rest of the body.

• We are so sensitive to other people's eye contact that even the slightest bit of it will cause the other person to notice your attention, at which point it will be too late to perform the scan.

What, you ask, should you look for?

Start by quickly noting how they're dressed. Ask yourself questions:

- Are their clothes expensive?
- Are they in style?
- Are they wearing anything that indicates a particular point of view or set of beliefs?
- Do they have any visible tattoos? If so, what do they show or say?

Also, pay attention to **The Big Four**:

- How is their body oriented?
- Are they using open or closed body language?
- Are they displaying any pacifiers?
- Do they appear to own the physical space around them, or do they try to take up as little of it as possible?

Another thing to note is their general energy level. Do they look confident and dynamic, or shy and insecure? We'll talk a great deal more about what confident body language looks like in a later chapter, but for now it's OK to just follow your intuition.

Finally, where is their attention focused? Is it focused outward or inward? If outward, then the body language you're reading is a reaction to things that *you* can easily observe as well. If their attention is focused inward, the body language they're exhibiting is a reaction to the thoughts going on inside their head. Generally, these thoughts relate to things that are happening in their lives, but you will not know specifically what they are unless you start asking questions.

The impact of the **Full Body Scan** comes from the fact that it forces you to become actively engaged in observing other peoples' bodies. It is not a passive process. You must not only pay attention to details, you must think critically about them. You must ask yourself the kinds of questions suggested. This will feel awkward at first, but after a few weeks, it will become second nature.

MIRRORING

In 2003, I was traveling from Chicago to Spokane, Washington for a show. I had an hour layover in Denver, but the plane landed just as a snowstorm was kicking in. The one hour turned into two, then three, and by mid-afternoon there was no telling when or if flights were going to get out.

I don't know what you do when you're in an airport and bored out of your mind. Most people read books. I read people.

There were three men sitting across the aisle from me. You could tell they all came from the same company because they all had on matching gray slacks and blue jackets.

Curiously, they were all sitting in exactly the same posture. They all had their legs crossed the same way, their arms folded the same way, their heads tilted the same way. It was so striking to me that I was amazed that nobody else seemed to notice it.

While I was watching the men, one of them uncrossed his legs. About a half-second later, the man to his right uncrossed his legs, and soon, like a domino falling over, the man on the end uncrossed his. I became transfixed. I had to see what they would do next.

Not much happened for about ten minutes. Then, without warning, the man in the center reached up to scratched his nose. By this point, my attention was starting to drift, but I caught the motion with my peripheral vision. Just as my attention shifted back to the men, the one on the left was reaching up to scratch his nose, and immediately following, the third man followed suit.

I recall thinking, "This has to be the ultimate example of mindless corporate conformity," when it suddenly dawned on me that I had just reached up and scratched my own nose! It turns out I wasn't immune to it either.

Whenever you find yourself in an airport, mall, or wherever you do your best people watching, spend some time looking at the postures of those who have gathered into small groups. Notice how many of them seem to have almost identical body language. They may have their legs crossed in the same way, their arms folded in the same way, their bodies leaning the same way. Sometimes they will appear to be mirror images.

What you are witnessing is variously called rapport or nonverbal synchronicity. Both names are just technical ways of saying that people who are members of the same group tend to mirror each other's body language. The precise mechanism behind this is only dimly understood, but it appears to be a way of subconsciously signaling to the others in the group, "I'm one of you; we're part of the same tribe."

This natural mirroring is a process that happens subconsciously. It's not as if people say to themselves, "Gee, I should move like the rest of these people." They just fall into the pattern without thinking about it.

Now that you are aware of this process, I can confidently make a prediction: You will be self-conscious for the rest of your life! Every time you find yourself in a group you will catch yourself mirroring, and you will have to fight the urge to think, "Stop it!"

However, I happen to think that people watching is fun, and I want you to feel that way as well. So, I'm going to teach you your very own "freaky mind trick" that you can play on unwitting members of the public. This is a detour from our more serious path of exploring mirroring, but it's a path worth taking because once you discover that this little trick actually works, you will be even more convinced of the power and importance of nonverbal communication.

Try this trick the next time you find yourself in a crowded place where people can see you, but aren't really paying a lot of attention to you; any place where you're just part of the background. It's ideal for parties, malls, airport concourses, or amusement parks.

- Spot an individual who is within 8 to 15 feet of you and start mirroring that person's body language.
- Adopt their posture. If their arms are folded, fold yours. If their legs are crossed, cross yours.
- Next, start to move with them. Wherever they move, however they move to be as close to a mirror of them as you possibly can.
- Don't make eye contact with them as you mirror them. There is, after all, a fine line between a freaky mind trick and a restraining order. But if you keep this mirroring up long enough,

you'll get to a point where you won't be able to tell who is leading the action and who is following. At that point, you get to take over. That person will follow your actions and have absolutely no idea he is doing so.

Obviously, you won't be able to get the person to move in huge ways; you're not going to get them to break dance or do jumping jacks. You'll get them to do subtle things, like touch their neck or play with a button. These are called "adaptors," and they're the kind of self-touch actions we all perform unconsciously throughout the day.

If you're highly ambitious, you can even try to set up a sequence of two or three movements and see if you can make them all happen. It's a shame that no one will know you're playing this game, because inside you'll be laughing like crazy!

There is, of course, a more serious reason we're discussing mirroring. It happens to be the most powerful way to establish a baseline for other people's behavior. What makes **Mirroring** so effective, particularly when compared with the **Full Body Scan**, is that mirroring not only forces you to pay attention to another person's body language, it also forces you to experience it. You're not just analyzing what they're doing; you're actually doing it along with them.

We all know from personal experience that when we feel sad or depressed, it feels as if the world's gravity has been turned to eleven. The weight of the world seems to be pushing us into the ground. Our bodies slump, and our legs and feet feel heavy. We're not only *metaphorically* "down," we're *physically* "down." On the other hand, when you are feeling happy and excited, it's as if gravity has been reversed. You feel light on your feet. You walk with a bounce in your step. Both your mood and your body language are "up."

The fact that there is a connection between how we feel and our body language is irrefutable. We experience it every day. If such a connection didn't exist, there would be no point even trying to read somebody. What you may not be aware of is the fact that the connection goes both ways. Just as changes in the way you feel affects your body language, changes in your body language can alter the way you feel.

Adopting more powerful, confident body language will actually make you feel more powerful and confident. If you adopt the body language of somebody who is nervous or fearful, you will soon feel that way as well.

The act of mirroring, then, serves two purposes:

•   You will clearly notice when something changes in another person's body language because yours changes as well.

•   Mirroring causes you to experience a version of the emotions they are feeling on a moment-to-moment basis.

> *The emotions you feel will likely not be as intense as theirs will be, but that's a good thing. Keeping a certain intellectual distance will allow you to remain a reasonably objective observer. And as you mirror someone's physical behavior, you will not only be relating to them on an intellectual level, you will be connecting with them on an emotional level as well. For me, it is the closest thing to "psychic phenomenon" I think is possible.*

A few tips on mirroring before we move on to other topics:

- First, although I use the word mirror, you do not actually want to mirror their behavior *precisely*. Unlike the mind trick I taught you, when you're mirroring to establish a baseline, you want to *approximate* their body language. If people catch on that they are being copied, they tend to feel like they're being mocked or ridiculed. That is not what we're trying to do.

- Instead of duplicating their motions precisely, try to be a little off. If you're sitting at a table with somebody, for example, and they lean in to confide in you, wait a few beats and lean in just half as much. If they lay an elbow on the table, try placing your hand down. Be subtle. Use this process to observe and understand. Your goal is to get in synch with them, not to ape them. Parlor games are fun and have their place, but put those aside when you want to make a real connection with someone.

- Finally, don't assume that body posture is the only way to mirror someone. I also suggest trying to mirror their breathing rate and the rate at which their eyes blink. Both of these are highly reflective of a person's emotional state. Paying attention to these seemingly insignificant details will make it almost impossible to miss when something has changed in their thoughts or feelings.

So, now you are observing how people physically behave. That should be about it, right? I just need to become a great observer, and I'll be an expert at body language!

In a word ... no. There is MUCH more to it than that – speech patterns and sound, clothing, use of time, color, etc. and they can be placed under the heading ...

V. PARALANGUAGE & BEYOND

Up to now, we've explored how our nonverbal physical cues communicate information to our listeners. But what about our oral cues?

As any English teacher will tell you, the specific words we use say a lot about our background, character, and life attitudes. This is true, but for our purposes, and the purposes of this book, we will be focusing on HOW we say those words. The tone, volume, emphasis, and voice characterizations of our spoken words—and even the pauses between them— communicate an equal amount of information, if not more.

This is known as **Paralanguage** (or above or outside language itself). Even though we all speak the same language, we each deliver it a little differently; one of your friends may be a fast talker who likes to use big words, while another may prefer to use short sentences and speaks loudly. If you are human, it is impossible to speak without paralanguage and, frankly, many animals use paralanguage as well! (Long-time pet owners will agree!) Every word is uniquely inflected with different volume and emphasis.

Therefore, paralanguage changes the meaning of your words – sometimes a little, sometimes a lot. For example:

- A thick accent that makes words unintelligible to the listener may impact the listener's opinion of the speaker.

- Utterances such as "like," "um," and "uh," are fillers, meaningless words (sounds, really) that act as space-holders while the speaker is thinking. A speaker who uses a lot of fillers normally projects low credibility.

- Even if your words are clear and well thought out, you can handicap yourself by slurring them, using slang, or inserting profanity.

- Deep resonant voices often command authority and reflect a higher status, while high-pitched voices, or low-volume voices, are often associated with lower status and weakness.

- Certain regional accents also deliver subliminal messages; British accents (in America) imbue a speaker with intelligence, while Southern accents often color the speaker as an intellectual lightweight. Of course, these are stereotypes, but they are hard ones to shake.

- You may also discover that you like or dislike a person who uses a large vocabulary and longer sentences, or the reverse may be true.

Very often, when we're misunderstood, we will change our paralanguage. We see this especially in non-English speakers, or people where English is a second (or third) language. When their listener is frustrated by their accent, or their lack of vocabulary, they often attempt to alleviate the situation by speaking more slowly, more softly, and more calmly. Their listener may or may not better understand them, but they will form a better opinion of the speaker - due to reacting to their paralanguage - and the likelihood of more effective communication is greater.

Example:

> *"Like, one of my least favorite, like, you know paralanguage quirks is like, when people use a word like, like, as a filler instead of pausing or, like, just adding in a word that doesn't, like, you know, mean anything -- know what I'm saying. OMG!"*

Enough! Some people (and some whole subgroups) create their own paralanguage, which effectively interrupts their thoughts and makes what they're saying practically unintelligible. *"Like," "Ya'know," "Know what I'm saying,"* and *"ummm,"* are among the most popular.

Many people are unaware that they use filler words. You, the reader, may be doing it, and are not aware of it, so here's a test.

> *Have a trusted friend listen to you describe something in your life (a memory, your living room, a favorite movie, etc.). Prompt them that if they hear you utter a "filler" word, they should call out your name. Each time they call your name, continue with your story, and try not to use another filler word. Hearing your name is memorable, and it will have a greater impact on you, as opposed to just having them clap their hands or say, "Hey." The results of this experiment may surprise you. If you are using a lot of filler words, you may now become more aware of them and, in the future, use a pause when searching for a word or thought. When you do, your speech will be clearer and less cluttered, and your listener will have a better "listening" experience. Eventually, you will start connecting thoughts more easily and fluidly. It's all about removing the ...um ... filler-word crutch.*

This exercise will help you become more sensitive to your own use of filler words, and to others as well.

DRESS AND OTHER TRIBAL MARKERS; IDENTITY, STATUS AND OUR SYMBOLS

Your choice of clothing, jewelry, and accessories sends a clear message of who you are, where you're from, and how you feel about yourself. Additionally, how you move, how you style your hair, and the scents you wear, also communicate a great deal about your personality, and affect how people absorb your messages.

Examples:

Envision a college classroom. A young man enters. He is wearing a sports jersey, a baseball cap (backwards) and sunglasses. He sits in a chair at the very back of the room, and immediately takes out his phone and starts texting.

From this description, what assumptions have you made about this person? What does he care about? Where is he from? What is he studying? What is his GPA, or his grade in the class?

Now envision the same classroom, and a girl walks in. She wears nice slacks and a blouse. She sits in the first row, opens a small laptop, and directs her attention to the Professor.

What assumptions have you made about her? What does *she* care about? Where is she from? What is she studying? What is her GPA?

These two examples are simple, if not stereotypical, but it's no mystery that as humans, we make these judgments—educated guesses, really—about others all the time. Here's another piece of reality—**so do your teachers!** (Yes, teachers are human beings.) Furthermore, teachers who are looking to achieve *maximum* success with *minimum* effort will often focus on those who look easy to teach and ready to learn. Is that you?

In addition to the obvious things clothes provide for us—protect us from the elements, flatter or emphasize our physiques, etc.—they can also be seen as "tribal markers." This is an anthropological way of saying something fairly simple—**the clothes make the person.**

They also can communicate some of the following:

- Economic class
- Job type
- Age (mental or actual)
- Sports team loyalty (often including geographical origins)
- Institutional loyalty
- Brand allegiance (and the social baggage that comes along with it)
- Political affiliations (or, at the very least, ideological affiliations)
- Our sense of humor or taste level

At the very least, our clothing places us within a societal group, and sends a personal message to those who see us. Of course, we can use this to our advantage. I'm sure you've heard the trope, "Dress for Success," or "Don't dress for the job you have, dress for the job you WANT." These are more than empty aphorisms—they reflect a very real situation.

Of course, there is no right or wrong way to dress—this is a free country—but it is important to realize that there *are* consequences to how we dress. It is not politically correct these days to acknowledge this fact, but the more your clothing and behavior connects you to a subculture, the more you will be associated with that group's dominant stereotype. Is this fair? No. Stereotypes fuel the worst kinds of oppression. But it is *real*, and awareness of it has the potential to give you a degree of control over it.

In addition, keep in mind that these "tribal markers" do more than simply identify you with a group: they exclude others. Since modern culture is becoming more inclusive and tolerant of "individuality," society, (at least American & European society), is much more likely to be accepting of individual quirks or "style." One way to counteract the divisive effect clothing can create is to make sure you are always displaying the nonverbal physical cues of openness, trust, and friendliness, especially when dealing with people outside of your chosen in-group. In other words, go the extra mile to show that you are approachable. Another way to control the situation is to vary your clothing choices and include symbols from many groups. This is not always possible when adhering to a dress code, but accessories and other accoutrements may help.

CHRONEMICS

Chronemics is the study of how we perceive and use time in nonverbal communication.

Time seems simple. It passes at regular (man-made) intervals and means the same thing to everybody, right? Or does it?

Consider the following:

- You are invited to a party that starts at 8 pm. What time do you plan to get there? 8pm sharp? Or will you plan on being "fashionably late?"
- Your class starts at 10am. What time do you plan to be in your seat, ready to go?
- You're taking a flight with a 7pm wheels up. Do you arrive at the airport at 6:55pm? Good luck with that.

As part of understanding body language, Chronemics becomes an integral part of assessing how or what we're communicating. It may seem like an awfully large leap to go from waving hello to the psychology of how we use time, but it's an important connection that helps us understand why our messages are being understood, or not understood.

Some regions (like New York City) communicate a feeling of rushed urgency derived from being a business-centric and over-crowded metropolis. Other regions, like Latin America, communicate a more laid-back attitude, with its inhabitants content to move and interact more slowly or deliberately. Neither is right or wrong, but it's good to understand that people across the globe have very different attitudes toward, and attach different levels of importance to, time.

Time is also a large indicator of status. A person may intentionally keep you waiting simply to flaunt their higher status. They may, in fact, do this unintentionally (this is called being rude!)—but the message is clear. They've demonstrated where in the social order they feel you sit, and where they feel *they* sit.

Status is also exhibited by the person who talks the most in a conversation or meeting, i.e. who takes up the most time.

Keep in mind that your time sense may be a barrier to communication. When you tell your mom, "I'll be right there," meaning you'll be there in 10 minutes, she may hear, "I'll be right there," meaning you'll be there in 10 *seconds.*" Clearly, this will cause a conflict!

Time is flexible, but it invisibly controls our paralanguage. You can't **see** someone's use of time, but their manipulation of it, regard for it, or disregard of it, can be **FELT**, and sometimes, that feeling communicates more than words or actions ever can.

"You may not remember what they said, but you will remember how they made you feel."

COLOR & COMMUNICATION

Most luxury cars are black, while most sports cars are red. The feelings that these colors communicate are unequivocal. Our language is littered with color references that communicate feeling; you feel blue, you feel green with envy, you see red, etc. It is not always consistent; nights are often metaphorically referred to as "black," while days are rarely described as "white."

Colors affect us in different, and interesting, ways. The psychology of color is an important part of nonverbal study because it can affect things like our moods, hunger, and even our level of excitement.

> *I've found adding color often increases the impact of my work. During my professional presentations, using a bright color ink on a handwritten note makes the message jump out.*

Here is a quick overview of what colors are thought to mean and how they affect people:

- **Blue** is seen as calming, like the sea or the sky. It is the most popular "favorite color."
- **White** has a variety of meanings. It is often seen as clean and sterile (like a doctor's lab coat); it is seen as cold and impersonal; it is the most common color for bridal dresses

(reflecting purity); in interior decorating, it will make a small space feel larger; in Latin, there are 7 different words for white, each with their own connotation.

- **Yellow** is a color of warning (think highway traffic signs) but it is also positive, relaxing and warm, like daisies or the springtime sun. It is said to enhance concentration.
- **Red** is both a warning color and one paired with passion (think red lipstick or Valentine's hearts.) It excites and stimulates. Many restaurants use red in their décor, menu, and logos because it is associated with hunger.
- **Purple** is seen as creative and a little off-the-beaten-path. It's normally used in feminine or creative endeavors. Purple is also regal, the color of royalty, and tends to stand out.
- **Pink** is widely considered a feminine color – men rarely use it, or when they do (remember power ties?) they use it in moderation.
- **Gray** is neutral and is often seen as boring, but it also communicates solidity, authority, longevity, and trust. It is the perfect banker's color, and the color of the military.
- **Green** is both calming and energizing – a good choice for painting a room (thus Green Rooms in theatres). It is commonly associated with plants and (in the US) money. As a skin tone, however, it says that someone is about to be sick.
- **Orange** is a color of warmth and warning. It creates urgency in the viewer.

- **Brown** is a bit dull, the color of dirt. It is associated with the earth and the natural world. It's a good choice if your product is "green."
- In art, **Black** is said to be the absence or negation of color, whereas visually (with regard to light), it is the unity of all color. Either way, it makes a powerful statement. It conveys seriousness, and sometimes, sinister intent. Common in the fashion world, it helps camouflage dirt. It's also considered slimming. It is also, in many cultures, the color of mourning and funerals.

The study of color psychology and communication could fill a separate book, but the take-away here is that the color choices you make—whether in clothing, automobile, paint, jewelry, binders & notebooks, etc.—sends a distinct message to others.

THE LANGUAGE OF TOUCH

Physical contact is an important part of nonverbal communication. Touch is often the first form of communication we experience. It not only includes our hands, but also our whole bodies, including the feeling of weight and temperature.

Touch can be overpowering or subtle, but there's no denying that human touch is essential to our happiness. It can be as brief as the brush of a hand, or as powerful as a kiss. Touch triggers fear, trust, warmth, and calmness.

Touching another person implies trust and a level of intimacy. This is why an unwanted touch is so jarring—we haven't given that person permission to contact us. Touch is as close as another person can get to us.

When exploring the power of touch, it helps to understand that some people are more touch averse than others. Think here of non-huggers vs. huggers. Part of a person's inclination to touch or hug depends on their gender, upbringing, and geographical location. Those from the Northern parts of the Midwest, for instance, tend to be more touch averse. Again, there is no right or wrong, just individual levels of comfort with person-to-person touching.

Touch is often controlled by protocol—as in a handshake—or limited to specific situations, like sports. Even when we accidentally brush against a stranger, we say "excuse me," apologizing for the violation of standard etiquette. American culture is more touch averse than many others. A handshake often represents the first, and perhaps only, touch you have with a person. However, after shaking hands, you may feel that you have greater leeway to make additional, socially appropriate touches with that person, but you must be very careful.

Here are a few general observations about how men and woman use touch:

1.   Women generally use touch more often than men.

2.   Men initiate touch with women far more often than they do with other men.

3.   Women initiate touch with other women far more often than they do with men.

We may attribute these behaviors to the fact that women may be concerned that touching men will be interpreted as a sexual signal, and they're right; men have a clear and proven tendency to misinterpret simple gestures of friendliness as signs of sexual interest. These observations also suggest that touch may convey a sense of power or control. After all, touching someone can be the ultimate intrusion into their personal space.

Men should be aware that when they touch women, especially those with whom they are not intimate, this touch may be perceived as domineering or sexist. This does not mean that touch cannot or should not be used, but to iterate, care should be taken to ensure that it is socially appropriate.

Touch plays many roles in communication, and like color, could have an entire book devoted to it, but here is a partial list of positive touch in communication:

- **Reinforcement:** A pat on the back or shoulder squeeze can mean, "Well done," or, "I'm impressed."

- **Direction:** A guiding touch shows a person—adult or child—the right direction to go.
- **Limiting or controlling:** Moms grab their kids before they run into a busy street.
- **Reprimand:** A touch of reprimand corrects behavior, often meant to shock rather than cause pain. Slapping someone's face is a strong example.
- **Comforting:** Hugs, caresses and similar touching helps sooth emotional and physical pain.

Of course, there are negative uses for touch, including punishment (a spanking), unwanted sexual touches, and sadly, violence.

We are constantly in physical contact with our world – we sit, lean, walk, lift and brush past things – and then react to that contact. Touch is so frequent, and so common, that we forget that it is always occurring. Our contact with the people around us, intentional or not, communicates something, and it's our job to try and control HOW we touch people, and WHAT information we want those touches to convey.

SPACE & DISTANCE

We mentioned this in an earlier chapter, but it's important to review the fact that personal space, and the distance at which we hold conversations, greatly controls that conversation, and how information delivered during it is received.

It is generally agreed that we have Five Zones of distance for the people in our lives:

The Five Social Distance Zones	
Intimate	0-6 inches (0-15 cm)
Close	6-18 inches (15 -45 cm)
Personal	1.5 to 4 feet (45 cm to 1.2 m)
Social (Business)	4-12 feet (1.2-3.6 m)
Public Space	12+ feet (3.6+m)

These zones refer to where we prefer people to be in relation to ourselves when we're talking with them. A long-term boyfriend or girlfriend is allowed "in close," probably in the *Intimate* or *Close* range, but strangers are allowed only in the *Social* range—4 to 12 feet.

The next time you're at a party, watch strangers having conversations; you'll most likely observe that most of the conversations are being held at the same distances. It's part of our collective training, culture, and expectations.

People have very clear ideas of what constitutes *their* space. This includes the space they actually own or control (such as their home or apartment), as well as the space they frequent— perhaps the same seat on the bus every day, or the same chair in the cafeteria. We all assume a casual ownership of these spaces because we use them frequently and we think of them as ours even though they are shared spaces.

We also use markers to indicate the space we control, sometimes laying a jacket over a theater seat to reserve it, or arranging a blanket on the grass or beach. Each marker indicates that this space is "mine," and you need to go elsewhere.

You can also use this as a tool to have an effect on specific people. By subtly invading, or threatening to invade, their personal space, you can put that person on edge, or cause them to become more alert or aware of your presence. Of course, you must be very careful because the consequences may not be what you intended.

IMPORTANT NOTE: Remember, if YOU can do this to someone else, THEY can do this to you, but that's OK. If you're aware that someone is trying to put you off your game by invading, or manipulating, your personal space, you now have a great deal of information about them. *Reading body language includes reading someone's attempts to read and influence yours.*

PRIVACY

An addendum to the study of social space is the study of privacy. There is a broad range of what we consider private, and with whom we share our private spaces. In basic training (in the military), you get to share a bedroom with 22 other men. This creates a sense of group identity. On the other hand, you may have visited a friend's home a dozen times and never once have you been invited to see their bedroom – it's a private space.

A good time to keep the idea of privacy in mind is when you are meeting someone socially or professionally. Is the meeting in their space, your space, or in a neutral space? This is important because it determines who is most comfortable, who will naturally be more in control, and who will most likely have the upper hand.

CULTURES, GENERATIONS, AND GENDERS—AND THEIR DIFFERENCES

This book is primarily about the American culture, but even within that controlled focus, there are many differences in how people perceive body language.

• Geographic differences: people in New York stand closer together than do people in Texas.

- Ethnic differences: Italians are known to speak with broad expansive gestures, and Lutherans in Minnesota tend to be reserved and quiet. Stereotypes, true, but often accurate.

- Generational differences: The primary objective of a new generation is to rebel against the last. Forms of dress relax, forms of speech change, the definition of appropriate physical contact evolves. This is on-going, so it's important when assessing someone's body language that you also note their generational identity.

TOE TO HEAD SCAN

We just reviewed several tools that support and inform the reading of body language, but on the next page there is a compact, step-by-step process you can use to assess nonverbal cues and paralanguage indicators.

The "toe-to-head" scan details many of the common gestures and movements seen in body language specific to North America. Global differences are vast.

Now that we've gotten a good start on understanding nonverbal cues and paralanguage - and how it communicates as much, if not more, than the actual words we use - it's time to explore how your newly-minted talent of reading body language can be used to improve your life.

Toe-To-Head Scan

Head: Common head gestures include nodding for "yes," shaking side-to-side for a "no," and tilted to one side for concern or "tell me more – I'm listening."

Nose: Scratching may indicate deception, or it may indicate an itchy nose. It is one of the body parts we point toward the thing in which we are interested.

Ears: Touching and rubbing for anxiety or lying, or perhaps and gnat is buzzing around them.

Shoulders: Slumped to show weariness or depression, raised in times of tension. Lifting both shoulders often signals, "I don't know" or "I don't care."

Hands: The hands are used for hundreds of gestures that communicate metaphorically (I am SO tired), or literally (It was this long") but no matter the use, they often reflect a person's mood; closed and tense in times of trouble; open when relaxed. Palms up or outward show an open and friendly message; a closed fist does not.

Feet: Feet often point in the direction of the thing we are interested in as well. Watch someone's feet to see who (or what) they are focused on in a room. We leak our nervousness or boredom there; often by tapping or twirling our feet.

Eyes: Staring at things that interest us. This could be worry or delight, or simply curiosity—context IS important.

Mouth: A smile can mean myriad things, but a frown is normally confusion, disappointment, or anger.

Neck: The neck is often exposed in flirting behaviors. This gesture is left over from our animal past when the more submissive animal would show his/her throat to the more dominant one.

Chest: The chest is often puffed out to look bigger for purposes of flirting and to make one appear more dangerous.

Hips: We tend to point to things we like or are interested in with our belly buttons. The hips are where you can very reliably see what a person if focused on – their "gut feeling," if you will.

Legs: Sometimes crossed legs are just a comfortable way to sit, but they can also signal a protective closure or nervousness. Wide open legs show comfort and also the claiming of a large personal space. (Or perhaps, someone's less-than-cultured upbringing)

Toes: Toe curl is a sign or either fear or pleasure

The "HOW" of Body Language

VI. LEADERSHIP

PART I: ARE YOU A LEADER?

You'd be surprised at the number of students who immediately answer, "No!"

During the course of your student life, you may be asked to run for President of a club, to organize an event, or to work to change a major campus policy. When you do, suddenly, without expecting it, you may discover that you are a leader. Now what?

Well, it's now your job to set an agenda and convince others to follow you.

However, holding an office with a title is far from the only time you will be required to demonstrate leadership.

• When you try to convince a person to go out with you, you're being a leader.

• When you try to convince a Professor to give you an extension on a paper, you're being a leader.

• When you try to convince another person to follow a course of action they otherwise wouldn't take, you are being a leader.

Granted, this assumes a rather broad definition of the word "leader," but for the purposes of this book, leadership is nothing more or less than the *act of persuasion.* The ability to

87

persuade—the ability to gain the cooperation of other people—is the single most important social skill you can possess. Whatever you've established as your life goals, you will need the help and cooperation of others to achieve them.

However, being a successful leader (read: a successful persuader) requires a unique set of skills, the most important of which is a command of nonverbal communication.

THE BODY LANGUAGE OF LEADERSHIP

In this chapter, we will look at body language skills that can help transform you into an effective leader. First, let's look at the personality traits required for leadership.

Answer these questions:

1. Why would you agree to obey or follow someone?
2. Why would you listen to them at all?

There are many answers, but for our purposes, three stand out. According to psychologists, you are more likely to follow someone if you like, respect, or fear them. That is leadership in a nutshell.

Each of these three attitudes is elicited in people as a result of different personality traits, which psychologists have labeled:

- Interpersonal Attractiveness
- Credibility
- Dominance

Each is a distinctive style of leadership, and we see examples everywhere.

INTERPERSONAL ATTRACTIVENESS

You may like a singer's stage presence so much that you want to buy his/her CD, or you may be drawn to vote for the most attractive candidate for school ombudsman.

TRUST

You might take courses that your faculty advisor suggests because he is a famous archeologist who has written books, or discovered the Crystal Skull.

STYLES

A teacher may threaten that you'll fail her class if you don't meet a deadline, or a coach may threaten to cut you from the team if you don't perform better on the field.

Each of these styles of leadership use specific types of body language. For example, in order for us to respect someone, we must first perceive them as both trustworthy and credible. They must look as if they have the knowledge and authority to lead, and that they have our best interests at heart. Body language that makes them appear untrustworthy or less-than-competent will undermine their ability to lead.

Others lead through their personal charisma. People follow them because their magnetic personalities create a desire to do what they say. This personal magnetism is communicated through the body language of confidence and authority.

Some people simply make us listen to them by sheer force of will. This "force of will" normally consists of a combination of physical and vocal factors.

Throughout this chapter, we will explore various styles of leadership and you will learn how to assemble a nonverbal toolbox appropriate to each.

BELIEVABILITY

Leadership involves not only communicating a convincing argument, but also projecting a convincing personage. The *content* of the convincing argument is up to you, but here are a few ways to project a convincing *appearance*.

Believability is crucial. No matter how convincing your idea may be, people will judge it through the lens of personal perception. In many cases, how you deliver the information will be just as important, if not more important, than the message itself.

It is human nature to evaluate an idea by judging its source. When we encounter a webpage or book, we immediately decide whether the source is credible by evaluating the author. Is the author respected by his or her peers? What are the author's credentials? What is the author's "good idea" track record?

Unfortunately, not all of our ways of evaluating an idea are valid. Our unconscious mind loves to take shortcuts, and we often—too often—judge the source by how they look, how they act, their social status, or even their race and gender.

You may think that you do not, or would not, fall prey to such obvious biases, but if you're being honest, you know that we all do this from time to time. In fact, entire industries have been built around our innate tendencies to make snap judgments on the basis of nonverbal cues.

If you doubt this, consider the following: how often do you see a television commercial for a new pharmaceutical product that *doesn't* contain a person dressed in a white lab coat? Almost never. The advertising industry knows that when you see that uniform, your unconscious mind immediately accesses a set of learned associations that makes you more likely to trust their product.

As a leader, you must always be mindful that everything you're trying to communicate is influenced and judged using the listener's personal scale of believability. Do you appear to be someone who has authority? Do you appear to be telling the truth? More often than not, these judgments are made unconsciously—based on superficial elements (manner of dress, body posture & position, accent, word choice, tone & cadence of voice ... remember those?)—rather than using empirical data (the actual logic or relevance of the information).

DOMINANCE

When people look at you, do they normally ask themselves, "Is he in charge here?" If they do, and if you have a desire to be a leader, you have an uphill climb.

Dominance is communicated through body language that displays authority. Yes, these visual elements are not always accurate, but most people, at least initially, tend to judge a person's leadership abilities by how well he or she conforms to a set of preconceived stereotypes.

For example, taller people are regarded, in general, as more authoritative, as are people with deeper voices. In today's American society, men are initially perceived as more authoritative than women, although that's rapidly changing. True? Fair? Not at all! Thankfully, these perceptions are gradually being relegated to "initial" reactions; experience and social mores are evolving our knee-jerk reactions. Unfortunately, they are often replaced with NEW knee-jerk reactions, but there is usually incremental progress. It will be a long time before they are eradicated altogether.

Here are some more. Caucasians are normally seen as more authoritative than non-Caucasians, and people whose clothing identifies them as having high social status are perceived as more authoritative than people whose clothing identifies them as having low social status.

Unjust? You bet it is! Does this make you angry? It should! In an ideal world we would never judge a person by such superficial traits, and indeed we should work hard to *not* do this. But the facts are undeniable, and are strongly supported by proven psychological research into our unconscious biases. These biases are ugly, they are unfair, and they exist in almost all of us, even if we are reluctant to admit it.

The good news is that there is a generational component to these biases; they seem to be less prevalent among the young. The bad news is, as I said before, they are far from dying out. Still, even though these biases exist in all of us, we must be aware of them so we do not allow them to control us. This is one of the *most* important reasons to study body language—to make ourselves consciously aware of what would otherwise be unconscious processes. Only by examining and overcoming our biases can we ever hope to make better, fairer, decisions.

There are many more nonverbal indicators of power and authority. The most obvious of these is … a uniform. We're all familiar with the uniforms worn by military and law enforcement, but the concept of "uniform" is more far-reaching. Uniforms appear in many walks of life, both professional and personal. The professor has his tweed sport coat, the doctor has her white lab coat, the executive has his "power suit," and the rapper had his baggy pants and bling. (Yes, those are as much a uniform as anything else!)

Larger people tend to be perceived as more authoritative, because size is associated with strength. Less eye contact, more deliberate movements, and fewer displays of emotion are also associated with authority and power.

 Authority is also conveyed through our posture. People in positions of authority more frequently use power stances and gestures. You'll see them standing straight, with their feet slightly wider than their shoulders, their head up, and their shoulders back. The wider than normal stance creates an impression of strength because the person is well balanced and difficult to knock over.

A common power stance includes holding your arms akimbo—having the fists on the hips with the elbows pointing out to the side. This image is so iconic that body  language experts tend to call it "The Superman Pose."

Postures that create an impression of authority tend to be those that command more space. The "Superman Pose," with the elbows jutting out to the sides, tends to make it difficult for other

people to get close. When sitting, a common power pose is to have one leg crossed over the other like the figure four. Another is to have both hands folded behind the head, again, with the elbows jutting out. Frequently you'll see a combination of the two. Both of these postures convey a sense of authority by claiming a larger amount of territory on behalf of the sitter.

All this talk of claiming territory brings us to another important marker of authority: position. This includes several diverse things, so let's start with where you sit. Leaders intentionally sit at the point of focus: the central chair, at the front of the room, or in the center of the group.

It's especially fascinating how a powerful position creates an aura of authority. In one study, researchers observed the interactions of groups sitting around a conference table. Later, when they surveyed the members about who they thought the leader

was in their particular group, the members inevitably said it was the person at the head of the table. This was true even though the subjects of the study were chosen at random and the people seated at the head of the table did not have any leadership training.

Perhaps the quickest thing you can do to gain authority is to stand up. Standing makes you taller, supports your breathing and enables the entire group to see you. People are forced to look up to you, which gives you a psychological advantage.

Another marker of authority derives from the fact that leaders normally demand the most desirable real estate: the closest parking space, the corner office, the top floor.

While posture is important, people also convey authority through movement. The common image of authority is one of a strong and steady figure. People in authority tend to be very clear in their intentions, and their movements and gestures are often expansive, focused, and deliberate.

Start monitoring your own posture and movements and limit unnecessary, unfocused movement. This indicates nervousness or lack of confidence. Particularly avoid the use of pacifiers and self-touch gestures.

It was my first ever college performance. The person who was going to introduce me was the president of the Campus Activities Board, and he approached me before the show to find out what I wanted him to say. I'll call him Paul, though it's been too long ago to remember his real name.

I gave Paul my introduction, which describes who I am, the television shows I've been on, and some of the highlights of my show. He asked me some further questions, and was so outgoing, so energetic, that I thought for certain he was going to do a fabulous job.

I was wrong.

Somewhere between backstage and the microphone, Paul made an astonishing transformation. In less than 30 steps, he switched from a confident twenty-year-old to a shy six-year-old. By the time he got in front of the microphone his posture slumped, his gaze turned toward the floor, his hands thrust into his pockets, and rather than reading the introduction in a firm, powerful tone, he mumbled the words in a volume just barely above audible.

> *Apparently Paul forgot (or his stage fright caused him to forget) that his job was to LEAD the audience. His job in giving the introduction was to draw a group of individuals together into a single, cohesive unit, and direct them toward a unified goal: enjoying the show.*

It may sound odd to regard public speaking as an act of leadership, but it is. As we've discussed, one of the primary tools of leadership is the control of body language. Just imagine how differently that introduction would have been had Paul walked confidently to the microphone, stood upright in a balanced, wide stance, made eye contact with the audience, and read the introduction in a strong voice rather than a hesitant one. The difference should be clear.

Even if Paul felt nervous on the inside (which is true of everyone in these situations), had he been in control of his body language, and used the tools discussed in this chapter, he would have been *perceived* as a leader, and the introduction would have been successful.

> *This small act of performing my introduction could also have brought Paul to the attention of important decision-makers in the room, and could have helped propel and further his college career. There is no such thing as a small opportunity. This was truly a missed opportunity for Paul.*

CREDIBILITY

Credibility is an amalgam of your believability, your perceived intelligence about a given subject, and your manner & delivery. The classic game show "To tell the TRUTH" put several panelists' ability to appear "credible" to the test every week.

"Credibility" is not just about competence or intelligence – it also includes how *honest* you appear. To some people, this comes very naturally, to  others, not so much. The often-frustrating aspect of this is, your perceived credibility may have very little relationship to your ACTUAL credibility—it's often based on the superficial factors we've been discussing. Again, it's not fair, but it's true.

Do people trust you? Do people think you have the knowledge and competence to get the job done when often, you do not? When trying to convince people of the validity of your way of thinking, not only does your *idea* have to appear believable, but *you* must appear believable as well.

In "The Chapter on Lying," we will explore how body language can be used to make people trust you. For now, let's discuss how body language causes people to perceive you as a capable, competent, and honest individual.

Paralanguage. Remember Paralanguage from way back in the good old days of the last chapter? You will appear more credible when you speak in short, direct statements. Your words should be clearly articulated and audible. On the flip side, when you speak with several false starts, when you use filler words, or when your statements end on a raised pitch that sound like questions, you are perceived as less credible. If you are experiencing these challenges, it is very helpful to write down what you plan to say and know your goal before you speak.

Action. Leaders by definition need to do something. Taking action, or at least being prepared to take action, is central to your credibility. This may seem simplistic, but leaders lead. Whenever possible, try to be at the front of a group. People look forward and up for leadership. Here's another important point: your credibility will soar if you appear willing to help with the work.

Emotion and Energy. Leadership is not just about projects but also about how we feel about and react to things. An energetic, excited leader will elicit similar energy from her team. The worried and cautious leader will, through mirroring, cause his team to be more worried and cautious.

Leaders show us what they think about the importance of an idea through their body language. If you present an idea with a sneer, obviously you are not in love with it. Attitudes are contagious, and the people you lead will often adopt yours.

The most powerful way to damage your credibility is through—what body language researchers call—*incongruence.* As we discussed earlier in previous chapters, **whenever there's a difference between what you say with your *words,* and what you say with your *body language*, people will often ignore your words and believe your body language.**

In short, your nonverbal cues must be consistent with what you're saying. If you go to a job interview "dressed for success," but your body language is weak and submissive, the interviewer will judge you by your body language. If you are leading a class project and tell your group that they need to be pumped up about it, but your voice sounds fearful and hesitant, they'll begin to doubt your ability to get the project done.

Modeling. Modeling is *demonstrating* the behavior we expect from others. A successful leader models timeliness, proper business clothing, and even speech styles

Modeling is used in teaching situations both consciously and unconsciously. It's a way of demonstrating expected behavior without explicitly spelling it out. Groups model behavior for other members of the group. You can easily witness this behavior by observing how members of a sorority or fraternity behave in social situations. How do they dress? How do they converse? How do they drink (or not drink) alcohol? With whom do they associate (or not associate)?

That was easy, wasn't it? It is clear that our nonverbal communication—as opposed to our actual words—is a more effective and powerful way to deliver a message.

Interpersonal Attractiveness. Why do we instantly like some people and not others? This factor is what psychologists call *Interpersonal Attractiveness*. Covering both friendship and romantic relationships, it includes several dimensions: physical beauty, similarity, reciprocal liking (we tend to like people who like us), proximity, propinquity,* and repeated exposure (we tend to like people more over time and repeated exposures).

Likability and warmth are often communicated through open body language, and additionally, people are judged to be likable if they are more animated and display greater emotion.

In general, the closer two people are in these respects, the more likely they are to be friends. Following this model, roommates are often placed together through the use of psychological profiles.

*Propinquity: how close, physically and psychologically, two people are.

Charisma. Charisma is the "big gun" in the room, and combines everything we've been talking about so far, especially being interesting and likable. You may initially think that "beauty" would be part of that equation, but experience teaches us that charisma normally has much more to do with energy, interest, and generating "like" in other people than it does with physical attractiveness. If a charismatic person is also physically attractive, that is a bonus, but it is not a requirement. Charismatic people generally have excellent social skills and use body language to build strong rapport and long-lasting relationships.

Actors and politicians are often said to have great charisma. All that really means is that people like them from the moment they meet them. Charisma is a general warmth and friendliness created by showing interest in other people, and not being focused exclusively on themselves. As a leadership skill, it is helpful to get out of your own head and focus on others. Sometimes a leader will sacrifice his or her time to help the greater good of the group.

HOW TO GET PEOPLE FIRED UP!

Getting people fired up about a project or an idea is an important skill for a competent leader. We, as individuals, tend to live inside our minds and focus on our own thoughts, but a great leader draws us out of ourselves and motivates us (and the crowd) to focus on a larger idea and act as one.

A successful way to accomplish this is to slowly build excitement throughout your presentation, and gradually raise your level of energy with your voice and body language. For example, over the course of a five-minute motivational speech, your voice may steadily become louder, your arguments may become progressively more persuasive, and your body language may become increasingly broad and more energized.

It also considerably helps to have a topic about which people care deeply.

> *I suspect there are very few speeches about car insurance that get people fired up. Although, in the hands of a talented speaker, I'm sure it's possible!*

If you wish to witness this behavior, take a trip to an athletic field, house of worship, or political rally. Getting people excited about, and committed to, an idea is a day-to-day activity for leaders in these situations.

GETTING THE BALANCE RIGHT

Leaders use many different strategies to motivate the rank and file. Some try to be everyone's friend, while others try to be as intimidating as possible. Choosing a successful strategy usually depends on the specific circumstances and the personality of the leader, but most studies identify two primary dimensions to leadership that can be reinforced by body language: likability and authority.

People are most easily motivated by those they like, or by whom they hold in a position of authority (or both!). We can see both of these dimensions at work in our own lives. We all know people we choose to follow because of their personal charm. We all know people we choose to follow because it is clear that they know what they are doing. Sounds easy enough, doesn't it? Just adopt the body language of somebody who is both likable and authoritative and you'll be fine.

Well …there is a problem with this. It turns out that the body language that makes you perceived as more likable *reduces* the perception of your authority, while the body language that causes you to be perceived as authoritative *reduces* your impression of likability.

For example, if a police officer pulls you over for speeding, you'll obey (learned behavior), but you won't be very happy about it, nor is it very likely that you'll have many "good feelings" about the officer pulling you over. From a body language perspective, the police officer is displaying all the nonverbal signs of authority: the uniform, the badge, the gun, the cruiser, and probably the physical postures and tone of voice. Each of these totems, if you will, is a reminder of how this person has the power to make your life very uncomfortable; their *likability factor* is very low.

However, if you remove these symbols, their likability factor will go up. Remove the uniform, the gun, the badge, and alter their tone-of-voice and physical presence to something more conversational and non-confrontational, this person transforms from a symbol into a human being, and subsequently becomes more approachable and likable. However, there is an obvious sacrifice of authority. (**NOTE:** Police officers are specifically trained to adopt an intimidating physical stance and tone of voice to ensure that they remain in control of all situations and keep themselves—and members of the public—safe. Remember this the next time you interact with a police officer and you'll have a greater understanding of what their body language TRULY means.)

The key to the body language of leadership is striking the right balance between authority and likability. If you lead strictly through authority, people will be willing to follow you in the short term, but over the long term, they will build up resentment and resistance to your leadership. If you lead strictly through personal charm, people will be willing to follow you when little is demanded of them, but they'll be less willing when you ask them to do something that is particularly challenging or risky.

Whatever your leadership style, and whichever dimension you most strongly exhibit, experts recommend balancing it with elements from the other dimension.

• If you come across as particularly authoritative, it is a good idea to make sure you adopt some of the body language that makes you appear likable. This way you won't come across as too domineering.

• If your leadership style depends on being a likable "buddy" type, it is a good idea to work on body language that demonstrates your authority and right-to-lead, particularly during crisis situations when people need a stronger hand guiding them.

In addition to striking the right balance between these two dimensions, it is crucial that leaders know which to emphasize. During times of stress and uncertainty, leaders should emphasize the nonverbal cues that convey strength and stability. When peoples' input is required, leaders should emphasize the nonverbal cues that convey warmth and likeability. People are more willing to participate when they feel their ideas are valued.

There is no single, correct mix of authoritative vs. likable body language when it comes to leadership. The right mix depends upon the demands of the situation and your own particular style. The important thing is to be adaptable. When situations change, so must your style of leadership.

THE IMPORTANCE OF CONFIDENCE

Confidence is the most powerful persuasion tool you possess. People are attracted to those who are confident and more likely to agree with them and do what they ask.

Again, there's a problem. Confidence is most important during challenging times, which, of course, are the times when you're often feeling the *least* confident; your palms start to sweat, your breathing becomes erratic, your body closes up, your mouth gets dry, and your thinking becomes muddled. It is a bit of a Catch 22.

So how can you avoid looking like the nervous wreck you actually are? Here are five simple tips:

1) ***Stand like an Army officer, only a bit looser.*** When people are nervous, they tend to draw into themselves, like a turtle withdrawing into its shell. Your hands will close into your body and your feet will draw closer together, which will affect your balance. When you're off balance, not only will you look more nervous, you'll feel it, too.

Widen your stance. Straighten your spine. Head up, chest out, shoulders back! Let your hands fall to your side.

This is how confident people stand: balanced, symmetrical, alert but not rigid. When you do this, you'll find an amazing thing happens. *You will not only look more confident, you will* **feel** *more confident as well.*

2)   **Move!** OK, I know you are thinking, *"Nervous people pace, don't they?"* When anticipating a stressful situation, nervous people do tend to pace. Except, when they actually meet that stressful situation, they tend to shut down. Think deer in the headlights. So remind yourself to change positions, but do it purposefully, and with a specific goal in mind.

3)   **SLOW DOWN.** Wait, didn't I just tell you to "move?" Yes, but move at a careful, measured pace. If you are nervous, your breathing rate may be elevated, and you will be inclined to move rapidly. To compensate for this, imagine that you are moving in a medium that provides some resistance, like water or molasses. Or imagine that you're moving like someone practicing Tai Chi. As you slow down you'll not only look more relaxed, you'll start to feel more relaxed.

4)   ***Find something to do with your hands.*** Fidgety hands betray our best efforts at looking calm, cool, and collected. Usually, in stressful situations, your hands will want to adjust or touch yourself in some way (pacifying behaviors, remember?). Think of Rodney Dangerfield tugging at his necktie.

Have you ever wondered why so many comedians and singers use handheld microphones instead of the headset type? One reason is that it gives them something to do with their hands. So if you are feeling nervous or fidgety, grab a pen and start taking notes, or pick up that coffee cup and take a sip. It doesn't matter what you hold, as long as it's motivated. In other words, don't keep picking up and putting down an object over and over again for no reason.

5)   **Breathe slowly and deeply**. When you're nervous your mind starts to prepare your body for a fight or flight situation. Your muscles will need more oxygen, so your unconscious mind sends signals to your heart and lungs to kick it up a notch or twelve. Your pulse goes up and your breathing becomes more rapid.

Deliberately start counting your own breaths. Inhale on a slow count of five, and let it out with the same timing. Continue to do this until you feel more in control of your breathing. When you inhale, do so deeply, taking in air all the way down to the bottom of your torso. Breathing in this manner will send a cascade of signals through your nervous system telling your brain it is OK to slow down.

PRESENTATION TIPS FOR LEADERS.

• Be clear on what you want from your presentation; define your goals. Whether you want the audience to elect you, laugh with you, or donate to the zoo, be clear. A strong focus helps alleviate nervousness.

• If you have limited time, work hardest on the opening and the closing.

• Use variety throughout the presentation. Vocal variety is important, but you should support your speech with a variety of body language signals—appropriate ones, of course.

• Great presenters almost always move around. If you watch a wonderful actor, speaker, or singer, they use the whole stage. However—and this is very important—they DO NOT move around aimlessly. They will move to one area of the stage, stop, and deliver a part of their presentation, then move to another area and continue there. Work out your movements beforehand, note them in your presentation, and then follow the notes. Plan the work and work the plan.

• Watching a person *read* a speech is boring. Even worse is "Death by PowerPoint," which consists of watching a person read text from an onscreen presentation.   Good presenters use gestures to *emphasize* their information, and they use PowerPoint to *support* their spoken words.

111

- Larger rooms require more volume and larger gestures. What may be appropriate for a meeting of six is lost on a group of three hundred. **Note:** If your microphone adequately amplifies your voice (meaning you don't need to raise your voice to be heard), retain a conversational tone, *but don't think that the microphone is making your voice more interesting;* if anything, an amplified voice requires more vibrancy and vocal variety to remain engaging.

- Eye contact connects you with the audience. When you catch different audience members' eyes throughout your presentation, you will create the illusion that you are speaking with everyone individually. This is especially important with large groups. Continually find different people in the audience whose eyes you can engage directly. You will appear more relaxed and connected to the group, as opposed to a person who is disengaged and simply talking over everyone's head.

This is also your most effective way to get immediate feedback. When you actually watch and observe an audience member's specific reactions to important remarks, you will immediately sense if they understand and agree with your message.

- People who are smiling, nodding, and looking at you are usually "getting it." Those who frown, look around, or look confused, might not yet understand your message (even though they may be trying). If you see a lot of wrinkled foreheads, they're not getting it. Address this – be open about it. Those people will be thankful that you cared enough to ensure that they at least understand what you are saying (even if, perhaps, they do not agree).

• Those who are checking email or texting are either too busy, don't care, or bored. These people are not your concern.

• Applause is great, but it's not the only form of positive feedback. Silence can also be an excellent sign; a quiet audience is an interested audience. However, they need to be *truly* quiet; coughing and fidgeting are signs that your audience is tuning you out.

MICROPHONES HELP YOU SPEAK WITH AUTHORITY

Keep in mind, speaking before large groups should be done on a platform, with proper lighting, and a microphone whenever possible. It is necessary to be both seen and heard to be effective. The more leadership roles you assume, the more often you will find yourself addressing larger groups. Plan to spend some time learning how to use a microphone.

As mentioned in the last section, a microphone is not a substitute for vocal variety—in fact, its use demands greater vocal variety. A sound system enables you to use more vocal subtlety and range, which is part of the paralanguage that conveys authority. Most speakers find it necessary to have amplification once the audience size grows beyond fifty. If you don't have a naturally strong voice, you should try to have amplification even when the audience numbers as few as thirty.

Also, in this day and age, many people have hearing challenges, and this is not relegated simply to the elderly. Slight amplification makes it easier for everyone to relax and understand what you're saying.

Don't forget, however, that your voice will sound a little different to the audience than it will to you. They're hearing your voice processed through the PA, while you're hearing both your natural voice and a slightly delayed, amplified version of yourself echoing back from the auditorium. This can be a little disorienting for beginning speakers. One way to alleviate this problem is to have monitors placed on stage so that you hear the same thing the audience does. If monitors are not available, slowing down your speaking tempo, and making your points a little more deliberately, helps you adjust to the echo.

Whenever possible, test the sound system before speaking. Walking around the stage while delivering a portion of your speech will not only show you which areas have the best acoustics, it will also make you feel more comfortable with the experience of standing on the stage. Your body language will reflect that comfort as you offer your presentation.

Lastly, when possible, have someone record your presentation, either using video or, at least, the audio. For first-time speakers, reviewing your presentation may be painful, but it is the BEST tool you can use—outside of a Director—to help you improve how you look, and how you sound. Eventually, you will notice GOOD things about what you did, and you will be able to repeat them in future presentations. This is how you grow.

WHAT TO DO WHEN THEY'RE NOT BUYING YOU

No matter how effective your leadership body language may be, there will be times when the people you're attempting to persuade just aren't buying it. You will be able to know this is happening by interpreting their body language.

Imagine you are sitting across the table from Michelle. You are running for Student Senate and you want to win her vote. As you make your case, you observe the following:

- Michelle folds her arms in front of her body and leans back in her chair.
- She also crosses her legs and angles her body slightly away from you.

These are not good signs. Michelle is exhibiting, as you recall, "closed body language." Both literally and figuratively, she is closing herself off to your ideas; she's resistant. This behavior is an unconscious manifestation of her desire to avoid discomfort. There is either something about what she is hearing or something about you that she does not like, so she tries to protect herself from the unpleasant experience.

The biggest challenge most of us face when somebody responds to us with closed body language is that we want to respond in kind. There are two reasons for this. First, we all have a tendency to unconsciously mirror the body language of the people we are speaking with. Second, we tend to view people with closed body language as being cold, hostile, or judgmental. We subsequently try to protect ourselves from these unpleasant feelings by closing off *our* body language.

This is the worst thing we can do because it creates a spiral of negativity and further alienates the person we're trying to persuade. The better response is to examine our own body language to make sure it is open and friendly.

Let's review. What does open body language look like? We'll start with the feet and work our way up.

- If a person is open to you, her feet are pointing in your direction. They are not tucked under the chair, but rather are on the floor in a comfortable position. If her legs are crossed, they are crossed in a comfortable, relaxed fashion. They are not crossed in a tense way, and, in particular, they are not tucked underneath the body. Typically, they are not crossed at all.

- If a person is open to you, her torso is facing you directly, not angled away from you. Likewise, her shoulders are squared toward you. Her arms rest comfortably, usually with the palms open toward you. Her face is also oriented toward yours.

• Her eyes are open relatively wide and focused on you. Her eyebrows are comfortably arched, and her expression is either neutral or a smile. From time to time she will nod or raise his eyebrows in response to what you say, signaling that she is listening and that she approves. Her body tends to lean toward you rather than away.

All of these behaviors have a powerful effect on your mood and attitude, even when you're not consciously aware of them. When a person's body language is open, you tend to like and trust that individual more.

It will feel awkward at first, but it is strongly recommended that you practice open body language in front of a mirror. Get a strong mental image of what it looks like to be open, and more importantly, pay attention to how your body feels in this position. Notice what parts of your body feel tension and what parts are relaxed. Then, whenever you start to speak with someone, remind yourself that you want to remain "open" to them, and try to relive the experiences you saw and felt while practicing.

It's also important to note that "closed" body language is not necessarily a response to your own nonverbal cues. It is entirely possible that the person is showing resistance to *what* you are saying, and not *how* you are saying it. In all cases, the first step to take when encountering signs of resistance is to check your own body language. At the very least, you can avoid worsening your communication problems, and at best, you may help the other person warm up to you enough that they are willing to discuss any objections.

VII. THE BODY LANGUAGE OF ROMANCE

For many of you, you turned to this chapter first. After all, we all have relationships in our lives, and our primary one (boyfriend, girlfriend, husband, wife, etc.) is one of the most important. Finding a partner is one of our primary life quests, and includes many tries, near-misses, and failures along the way. Seeing – and sending – the right body-language signals during this journey can help you get more dates, and better understand potential partners.

Most students are primarily concerned with *starting* a romantic relationship, and body language plays an important role in this process. You may already be able to read some of the obvious cues that indicate romantic interest on the part of another, but you also need to be aware of the cues YOU are throwing out – and know how to avoid sending signals that suggest you are unavailable or not interested. You must also be able to know when your cues aren't being received or understood. When you can do this, you will be able to modify your behavior so that "special someone" finally gets the hint. In this chapter, we will explore how to identify and send the right messages to a potential partner.

NOTE: The body language used to kindle romantic interest is only part of the equation. Once a romantic relationship has begun, it is maintained largely by nonverbal communication, which is true of most of our relationships. Our body language continually tells the other person whether or not they are important to us, who the dominant person in the relationship is, whether we are truly paying attention to them, and if we care more about them than about ourselves.

As a student, you will meet and interact with many people. Which ones are available? Which ones are interested in you? Which one are most *like* you? Dating, for the purposes of this book, is defined as *the process of transitioning from friend status, to a romantic status.*

BEFORE WE GO ANY FURTHER ...

... let's be clear on one thing: "No" means No. Every time, all the time. The dated, old saw, "her lips tell me no-no, but there's yes-yes in her eyes" no longer has any validity in our society.

That said, sex is often the number one extra-curricular activity on many campuses. It is often the first time, or at the least the first significant time, most student experience sexual relations. The cues that most people misinterpret at this stage are the ones that indicate "you may go farther" – most of which are nonverbal.

There are a series of steps that take you and your partner from clothed, upright strangers to naked, horizontal lovers and we need to be very clear here:

You may not push, coerce, threaten, trick, or in any way force someone do what you want. You need the other person's agreement and permission.

Otherwise it's rape.

Consent is mandatory; this means that the other person must be a willing partner and is happily engaged in a sex act with you. This is essential emotionally and legally.

MOVING ON

Now that we've set some ground rules, let's move on to a discussion about constructive romance and relationship-building.

The tips and techniques outlined in this section are designed to help people read their intended partner's "signs," but we'll begin with a general observation that to many is obvious, and to some, is NOT so obvious.

When it comes to being sensitive to romantic body language, most men are clueless.

A generalization, you say? Consider this:

First, the question asked most frequently by students is, *"How can I tell if **she** is interested in me?"* Note the pronoun, "she." The question is rarely, *"How can I tell if **he** is interested in me?"* Males are clearly more in need of guidance in this area.

Second, when a woman asks about romantic body language, it's typically something to the effect, *"Why doesn't he pick up the signals I'm giving off? I couldn't be more obvious!"*

Trying to read your romantic (or potentially romantic) partner's signs can be intimidating, and is normally attempted when you're at your most vulnerable; namely, when floating in a fog of infatuation. This is not the time when you do your best work.

However, what follows is the #1 most effective way to learn EXACTLY what another person is thinking at any given time.

Ready?

Here it comes … it's really awesome …

… ask.

That's right; if you're not sure of what a person wants, needs, and desires, simply **ask them.** You'll be surprised at how effective this approach is. This isn't to say that it will definitely open doors that were previously closed, but it *will* reflect well on you should romantic interest ever arise (so to speak).

Who knows, the answer may be "yes," and doesn't THAT save time!

Of course, whatever the answer is, listen to it and accept it. People do not owe you a detailed explanation. The clues to proceed with a sexual encounter are often a mixture of verbal and nonverbal agreements. The nonverbals may include permission to be in an intimate space with you, free physical contact, open (in some cases *very open*) body language, reciprocation of kisses, touches, etc., and continual positive reinforcement (such as "Yeses" and smiles). There are *many* messages flying around in these situations, and your hormones will have shifted into overdrive, so you may misread things. Therefore, if you have *any* doubt, ASK, and all will become clear.

Second note for guys:

We biologically tend to be bigger and more sexually aggressive than women. I emphasize the word "tend" because this is certainly not true in every case. However, a six-foot tall man standing in front of a five-foot tall woman is going to be intimidating no matter how gentlemanly you are. And "fear" is not the emotion you're trying to invoke here.

Males—especially taller & larger males—need to moderate their behavior to take this into account.

- Be aware of her spatial needs.

- Stand back a bit more, or off to the side and don't tower over a partner.
- Perhaps sit down, so you can be more on her eye level.
- Allow her a larger bubble of personal space until *she* moves to close it up.

Be aware that personal space is very important, especially early in a relationship. Personal space will be explored more thoroughly in another chapter, but a relationship can be characterized as a journey through another person's personal space and comfort levels until intimacy is reached (or not reached). In short, initial meetings are always a good time to *literally* take a step back.

THE STEPS OF ROMANTIC ENGAGEMENT

Animals engage in a variety of mating rituals, some of which are quite elaborate. When it comes to the body language of romance, it's helpful to think in similar terms. We can break down the process of romantic attraction into steps, with each one having become ritualized.

Many sociologists have attempted to chart these steps. Some have defined as many as a dozen, but for our discussion, there will be four. This should help make the process of courtship more understandable.

A great list was developed by Psychiatrist A. E. Scheflen in 1965 (A.E. Scheflen, Quasi-Courtship behavior in psychotherapy. *Psychiatry,* 28, 245-257). He broke the process down into these four steps:

1. Courtship Readiness Cues

2. Preening Behavior

3. Positional Cues

4. Actions of Appeal (or Invitation)

These are very effective ways to summarize how we as a species, and a society, approach romantic relationships.

1. __Courtship Readiness Cues__

The first type of body language we engage in is categorized as a "get ready" phase. This is when we know we're going to be on display, and we want to present the best product we can. Physically, we'll sit up straighter. Men may suck in their stomachs and hold their heads higher and squarer; these are stereotypical masculine behaviors. A man's voice may also reflect a "readiness" cue; he lowers the pitch of his voice to make it sound deeper.

For women, this "get ready" phase typically involves adopting more stereotypically feminine behaviors. Vocally, a woman may pitch her voice a little higher or deliver her remarks more gently, use softer, more feminine gestures, hold her chest out, and sit or stand in a flattering position.

For both sexes, the selection of clothing is also extremely important during this phase, and there are many factors to consider, with each sex determining the right blend of physical flattery and status. After all, clothing can make a woman appear sexy and elegant, or cheap and trampy. What she chooses to wear depends on her goals and the psychology of the target audience. If a girl is planning on going to a nightclub to have a quick fling, her clothing choices will be radically different than if she were going to a church social, or looking for a long-term relationship.

The same applies to men. Men have a reputation for being clueless when it comes to fashion, but they still (successfully or not) will try to select clothing that flatters their physiques and hides their flaws, while deciding whether to appear casual or formal. And these days, there are *many* men who are quite stylish and have great style sense (sometimes, better than woman), so even those stereotypes are quickly eroding.

But a guy's clothing choices during the "get ready" phase also communicate a great deal about how he sees himself and whom he's trying to impress. These choices also communicate his level of self-awareness. Some may choose to wear a sports jersey in order to look athletic, while another may choose a neatly pressed dress shirt and tie to appear wealthy and sophisticated.

2.   Preening Behavior

The second phase is the "preen." This is when either sex makes the final adjustments they feel are necessary to look their best and attract a mate. Women may adjust their makeup, play with their hair, or possibly undo a top button or two. If men are dressed more formally—wearing a suit or tie—adjusting their clothing to hang properly will be a major pre-occupation. Since most men today tend to dress more casually, preening has become a more subtle activity, and is usually limited to adjusting their hair. And if they don't have much hair to adjust (either by choice or by Mother Nature), this preening behavior may be focused on the little that's there. And if a guy has facial hair, he'll tend to spend a fair amount of time and attention getting it to look just right.

3.   Positional Cues

After the preening phase comes "positional cues." This is where each player in the game is positioning his or her body to signal that he or she is ready and interested in receiving romantic attention. If the player is out with friends, for example, they will start to separate themselves from the rest of their group. Sometimes this can be subtle.

Imagine, for example, a group of women at a bar, chatting and laughing. Most of their eye contact is on one another, but one woman has turned her head away and is starting to scan the rest of the room with her eyes. Sometimes, the separation is more overt.

If an individual is alone, positional cues could include a straighter, more alert posture, more open body language, and an orientation away from obstructions, like a wall or the bar. When two people are close together, and one is the object of the others interest, the positional cues will feature the pursuer adjusting his or her body to give that person more exclusive attention and to block out possible distractions, such as advances from romantic rivals.

4. <u>Actions of Appeal (or, The Invitation)</u>

The final class of body language associated with the courtship dance is the "Actions of Appeal," or put more simply, "The Invitation." The most powerful component of this is eye contact. The person offering the invitation will hold a gaze for significantly longer than they normally would.

Of course, "invitation" body language can and usually does go far beyond greater eye contact. In a woman, the gaze is typically accompanied by flirtatious smiles, self-touch like curling one's hair, or stroking one's own neck. For a man, it may include flexing a bicep or puffing out the chest in an attempt to look stronger or more masculine. Brief or 'accidental' touching may also accompany this step on both sides.

One notable type of "invitation" body language can be characterized as "framing your dirty parts." At this point, both men and women will frequently adopt postures than call attention to their sexual assets. Women will often fold their arms under their breasts to lift them and emphasize their cleavage, or they'll stroke their thigh in a way that draws attention to the 'promised land.' Men who are standing will often adopt a "fig leaf" pose; they'll stand with their thumbs tucked into their pockets and their fingers forming a sort of picture frame around their crotch.

What makes framing behavior so amusing is that in most cases, it happens unconsciously and the participants don't know they're doing it. At the same time, the other player in this game is seldom consciously aware of their behavior either. So, you simply get to watch the nonverbal show! Even though the players aren't aware of the cues, their unconscious minds are picking up on them and those cues continue to perform their special magic.

Here is another way of looking at this courtship dance:

STEP ONE: CONTACT

You see a person who appeals to you ... and so it begins. The first thing to determine is; are they interested and available?

Signs they *aren't* available:

- Hanging out with the same person the whole time.
- Frequent insertion of the words "girlfriend" or "boyfriend" into their conversation.
- The presence, on the left hand, of a wedding or engagement ring (OK, this person may still be very interested— and for some the ring adds to the allure—but this book does not promote home-wreckers, male or female.)
- They ignore you completely.

Signs of possible interest:

- They glance at you frequently, or stare at you.
- They display flirtatious behaviors.
- They orient themselves toward you, or include you in the group by making space at a table or conversation circle.
- Smiling, especially when looking directly at you
- Casually touching you on the arm or other non-sexual area.
- A raised state of energy or excitement when you show up.

As an experiment, watch one of your friends before, during, and immediately after his/her significant other appears in a room. You will most likely witness all of these behaviors in quick succession. Or, and this is the risk you take when observing people, they may NOT display any of these behaviors, and this could mean you are witnessing a relationship in trouble.

The Approach

When approaching someone in a social setting, keep in mind that you are an unknown. They will start making guesses and assumptions about you from the moment they see you. Simultaneously, you are trying to lower their defenses, reduce their fears, create a sense of interest (in you), and demonstrate that you are open to *their* interest, all in just a few seconds. That's a lot to remember, so...

When approaching, remember: SEO

S= Smile

E = Eye contact.

O= Open body posture

These things will help you to look nice, warm, approachable, non-threatening, and cool – all things that make you dateable. Or at least—at this stage—conversat-able (if that's a word).

It's wise to not surprise people by suddenly invading their space, so try this—let them see you at a distance and then enter their space slowly. Then say "Hi" and watch their cues ... if they look away, or frown, or spit up blood – well, it's not meant to be. However, if they stop what they're doing, smile, and turn towards you, those are good signs.

The idea behind dating (apart from the obvious reason) is to find someone whom you like, who likes you back, and with whom you wish to spend time (and likewise, them with you). Your success rate is often highest with people who have interests, values and goals that are similar to yours. The "work" of dating, then, is to seek and identify sameness and compatibility; do you share common interests, beliefs and goals?

During this initial contact phase, you will learn a great deal about the other person, which could take a few hours, days, weeks, or months. NOTE: The time it takes to learn about a person is in inverse ratio to their openness and willingness to be "discovered" by you. Sometimes, you need to take the hint.

STEP TWO: BODY POSITIONING & TOUCH

In personal relationships, be aware of where you stand – literally. As mentioned earlier, I characterize dating as the steps taken to close the distance between two people. (See notes on the nonverbals of personal space.) At the beginning stages, you are an unknown, just past being a stranger, and you will be "invading" their public and conversational spaces.

Outside of the most unlikely or alcohol-fueled situations, you will not be able to skip steps – such as jumping from conversational distance to intimate space in the first few minutes. It just doesn't work that quickly. You need to wait until you are both comfortable enough to let the other person into your own personal space. This may happen at different times, and at different rates, so you need to be aware of each other's timetable. In fact, you may move forward and back in the zones—literally and figuratively—until the other person is ready to allow you to move closer and occupy their personal world.

STEP THREE: EXPLORATION

Now you've moved past initial observations, and are seeking to learn more about each other; what you like, what you know; your upbringing, etc. "Dates" are really just chances to interact and explore the other person's world – what they do, what they like, and their personal beliefs.

While many early dates are activity-based—going to a movie, bowling, or going to a party—there are two key skills that are very important; listening and mirroring (See "Mirroring", page 56).

The majority of couples will need to go on several dates before they know if they like each other enough to take things to the next level. There are many social rituals involved with dating: sending flowers, who should call whom, how soon should they call, and which half should initiate next steps. Feel free to observe, translate, or ignore these at will. They will be completely subjective to your individual relationship.

STEP FOUR: GROWING INTEREST, INTIMACY, AND THE DISCOVERY OF DIFFERENCES.

During this step, you'll spend more time together, and will develop deeper feelings for one another. Generally, you both enjoy each other's company. Your conscious and unconscious behaviors may begin to include spontaneous smiles when they appear, hugs, close personal distance, and talking about the other person more often with your friends or family. There will also be differences you discover ... no two people are exactly alike. At this point, you will begin to understand how this person is different from you, and if, despite these differences, you can get along.

STEP FIVE: COMMITMENT

You are now dating exclusively, having made a commitment.

A couple having reached this stage is in very close proximity, often touching and sharing a "private vocabulary" of words, experiences, and actions. In its most extreme form, they are oblivious to the world around them, and are focused solely on each other.

They may sit next to each other, touching hips and arms, or they may sit opposite each other but take up very little space while doing it, exhibiting lots of eye contact. They may also exhibit minor (or major) public displays of affection.

A commitment can be long term or short term, and can be marked in several ways, the most obvious being marriage and a wedding ring. It shows society that this person—the ring wearer—is in a committed relationship. It is one of the simplest cues for a student of body language to notice and read. There are other ways to see that a couple is together as well—hand-holding, kissing, sharing of clothes, cohabitation, or something as simple as always attending social events as a couple.

MAINTAINING A LONG-TERM RELATIONSHIP

Relationships are sustained through attention and listening. Time is very important; and it is extremely difficult to maintain a relationship if you do not devote time and attention to it. In addition to the quantity of time you spend with someone, the *quality* of that time is equally, if not more, important. Your nonverbal cues should demonstrate to your partner that they are at the center of your attention and that you are truly paying attention to what he or she is saying.

While I recommend mirroring at all times, it is particularly important in maintaining intimate relationships. Couples who are truly close continue to mimic each other's body language. Couples often interact face to face; they look at each other and listen. Of course, outside events can become distractions. These include watching screens of all kinds, listening to loud music, or other background activities that shift your focus away from your partner. Clearly, these should be avoided, and here's a simple first step; when talking with someone who is important to you ... turn off your phone! Or, if you need to keep it on so you don't miss an important call or text, acknowledge this and perhaps apologize in advance. This lets the other person know that you value this interaction and regret any distractions.

In another chapter, we discussed the importance of touch. Affectionate touching is one of the ways we maintain our intimate relationships. When couples stop touching one another, it's generally a sign that the two are drifting apart emotionally.

Few relationships make it to the stage of becoming a primary relationship. You will likely date many people on the way to finding a great fit. Think of it as a way to meet lots of new people and practice your body language skills

THE KISS-OF-DEATH

There are several types of body language that are the kiss of death to most relationships. One is the facial expression of disdain. Another is body language that makes a person appear untrustworthy. Relationships are built upon trust, and if one partner is lacking that, there's very little, if anything, that will repair it.

A brief side-note on sex (the intimate kind, not the gender kind.)

While this is definitely a PG book, it's interesting to note that the steps to having intercourse are a series of verbal and nonverbal cues and permissions as well, and it is VERY important to read them correctly.

Sex is exciting, hormone-charged, and often confusing, especially with a new partner in the early stages of a relationship. If you are unsure about what your partner's nonverbal cures are saying, you can fall back on the advice offered earlier in this chapter … ask. ("What would you like to do now?" "Does that feel good?")

WHAT IS OBSESSION?

Obsession (or stalking) is a psychological malady where a person cannot, or WILL not, recognize the signals that their potential partner is not interested in them. Of course, many of these "signals" may be unfettered vocal reprisals telling the "stalker" to stop contacting them, etc. Part of being a skilled communicator is noticing when your interest signals are not being returned, or if they're being returned *much* too easily, quickly, or in any way, irrationally. Therefore, if, after a few dates, the other person is exhibiting unstable behavior, well, perhaps it's time to move on.

OLFACTICS

People forget that we are biological organisms. We like to think that we are advanced beings who are in control of ourselves and the world around us.

The fact is ... while we are, indeed, highly functioning animals ... we are still ANIMALS. And one of the areas where this becomes evident is in the science of Olfactics – communication by smell.

Most people regard perfume as an attractant, and leave it at that. The science of Olfactics is much more than a flowery scent to attract mates, or a musky one to attract females.

There are two components to smell – pheromones, and everything else

Pheromones are the chemical cues that people send out. Yes, we transmit chemical information all the time. If you think to yourself, *"That's interesting, but I've never noticed myself emitting pheromones,"* it's because you can't perceive them consciously. Pheromones operate on a person's emotional brain, and they influence your actions without your being aware of them.

Scents act in four major ways

1.   Attraction
2.   Repulsion

3.   Memory

4.   Hunger

Smell is one of our most primitive senses and it influences us more than we like to admit. Smells attract us to food, flowers, and even partners, and repulse us from unhealthy things. (Imagine the smell of spoiled food in your fridge.) Have you ever noticed that when you have a cold and your nose is stuffed up, your food doesn't taste the same? This is because smell is a very large component of taste. Smell is also a powerful memory trigger reminding us of times, places, and people, and can even transport us, emotionally, to those situations.

Similarly, when you meet a new person, you may think, objectively, they look quite attractive, but there's just "something" about them that isn't clicking with you. Likewise, you may meet someone who you think does not conform to your "type," but you find yourself powerfully drawn to them. This is very likely pheromones at work. You are chemically very compatible with this person.

Finally, smells are tied directly to hunger; smelling desirable food triggers the hunger reflex.

In North America, it is not OK to smell bad. We find body odor, bad breath, and some strong food smells (garlic, onions) unappealing. We spend a great deal of time and money removing or masking these smells. Whole industries are built upon the goal of sanitizing our lives, and replacing unpleasant smells with more pleasant ones.

Keep in mind, however, added scent is supposed to be subtle, not alarming or all encompassing. If you're using perfume, or something like Axe body spray, please use it in moderation.

SUMMARY

In the final analysis, dating – and personal relationship building – is probably the most complicated aspect of human interactions. Business relationships have - at the very least – a fairly standard set of shared processes and goals. Yes, each relationship has its own individual quirks, but in a business relationship, both parties can safely *assume* that all parties want the relationship to be successful financially and professionally. Why else would they enter into it? If there is a hidden agenda, however, that will normally become exposed at some point, and one of the parties can deal with it … or not deal with it, as the case may be.

In romantic relationships, on the other hand, there is rarely a well-defined set of goals established up front that are ***known and shared by both parties***. Note the emphasis; both parties may have well-defined ***personal*** goals in mind, but they are usually unspoken, if not kept intentionally secret. And this is where the reading of body language can help.

By understanding and interpreting a person's nonverbal cues, you may be able to determine if what *they're* thinking and feeling aligns with *your* goals and desires – even if nothing is ever discussed openly. Furthermore - and this is where it gets a little spooky and fun - you may be able to learn something about a person that they themselves don't understand. Yes, that's right. Attraction (or aversion, for that matter) is not necessarily intellectual; it's usually much more influenced by emotion and chemical processes - the Caveman Brain – remember him? It's this leaking of information that will enable you to adjust your own behavior, which in turn, will give you a measure of increased confidence.

And that's what it's all about. To paraphrase a famous quote about real estate, *"What are the three most important things about being successful in romantic relationships? Confidence, confidence, confidence."*

This chapter, along with the rest of this book, has been designed to school you in the fundamentals of body language, and to help build the confidence you need to create happy, healthy relationships.

Now that you have mastered the Art of Romance (!), t's time to apply yourself to more important matters … homework.

Of course, "important" is a relative term, but it must be assumed that you are attending college to gather the skills you need to succeed in the real world. A specific goal during your college career should be - and if it isn't, it **should** be - increasing and strengthening your professional opportunities (internships, appointments, mentorships, etc.).

This brings us to the next chapter.

VIII. THE BODY LANGUAGE OF BETTER GRADES

If you change your nonverbals, you can, in many cases, improve your grades.

Wait? What?

When researching this book, this was, perhaps, one of the biggest surprises to surface. *Where* you sit in your classroom, and *how* you act, can affect your grades. It shouldn't be surprising to note that your teachers and professors will be affected by your nonverbal communication. Of course, you will be affected by THEIR nonverbals. The *most* surprising thing is that your nonverbal behavior choices, in the classroom or in your lecture hall, can change your *own* level of attentiveness, and therefore, your grades.

This is one of those decisions that you make early on in your college career—whether you will attend every class, if you will always (try to) be on time, and where you will choose to sit. As it turns out, these choices are very important.

There are several factors to consider when you attend a class, and each can affect your level of learning, and therefore your final grades. Let's look at them briefly here.

WHERE TO SIT

Where you sit in a classroom or lecture hall will affect how you are perceived by teachers and fellow students alike, and how you interact with everyone. Imagine a lecture hall, and then visualize a triangle, the top of which is front and center, with the sides radiating out toward the middle of the room. Students sitting in this zone will interact with the class more, and will subsequently receive better grades. Yes; better grades by choosing where to sit!

Sitting in the front row is even better–there are fewer distractions, you can see and hear better, and you will naturally interact more with your professor. Conversely, sitting farther back in the room provides the opportunity to arrive late and leave early. You may never intend to do either, but your teachers will perceive that you could *possibility* do this, and this perception isn't optimal. It's very subliminal, yes, but it's also very real. Since some professors assign grades for participation in class, its best to sit down front, participate, and get remembered.

Studies have shown that for every row back from the front a student sits, that student will experience a 0.1 point drop in their G.P.A. Now, these studies do not take into consideration the variables that better students may tend to sit in the front naturally (skewing the results), or that students may, by default, become better students because sitting in front causes them to be more engaged, but the study still offers valuable information. Additionally, you may wish to avoid the extreme front left and right seats in the front rows, as they may fall outside your teachers gaze, reducing the benefit.

- Three benefits of sitting up close:

➤ Increased interaction

One of the reasons to sit front and center in the classroom is that not only can you see the instructor and the materials better, but *they* can also see *you*. One of the best ways to engage your brain – and to help you understand new material – is to ask questions. After all, learning, even in the lecture hall, is interactive.

➤ A better relationship

Sitting down front, having good posture, and practicing active listening, may also help you connect with your professor. They will notice you (and be in closer proximity to you) which may lead to professional opportunities, such as an internship. After all, teachers are more likely to pick active, interested students for these roles.

➤ "A little help on the test..."

One interesting part of body language is that we can often learn when a person – your teacher in this case – is excited by a particular topic, and what they consider to be important, and thus more likely to be on the test. Some professors even have particular "tells" … actions that give away these important moments. If your teacher pauses and points at the class, it might be to emphasize a key point. Pay attention to what is emphasized, repeated, and written down. Eventually, you won't need to ask "Will this be on the test?" Their body language will give it away.

➤ Your posture and dress

A simple rule applies here. People who look serious are treated more seriously. For example, a woman arriving for class early, wearing a nice blouse and dress slacks, is seen as someone who is paying attention and who wants to learn. Conversely, another woman who arrives to class wearing sweat pants, an old tee-shirt, and a backwards ball cap, is not going to be seen as a serious student.

> *Yes, I know that this categorization—or generalization, really—is very often completely inaccurate, but it is more than likely this is how these two people will be perceived. I suspect—no, I KNOW—that there are great students who slouch in the back row wearing their jammies. They, however, are in the minority.*

Have you ever noticed that it's hard to sleep standing up? That it's also hard to pay attention lying down? That it's hardest of all to take notes from a beanbag chair? Along these lines, maintaining a focused posture and proper dress helps you pay attention. It's always amazing to see students fast asleep in the back row; ostensibly, they chose to be in this class, and more importantly, they are paying to be there, or, in this case, sleep there.

NOTE: Making eye contact with your teacher tells her that you are paying attention and are interested. Making eye contact with your text message or laptop does not.

CHRONEMICS

Yes, you may have to change your relationship with time–and it *is* a choice. You may have been a laid-back surfer dude in high school, and refused to wear a watch on the basis of your personal philosophy; "I'll get there when I get there." You will find that classes, events, and especially tests, normally start right on time.

There may be no scientific evidence for this—primarily because it's fairly self-evident—but there is very likely a strong correlation between going to every class every day and being on time, with getting higher grades. In much the same way, if you are a procrastinator, it might be time to change your ways and use your time more wisely and efficiently. While it may be possible to write a paper or read a book overnight, you will not learn as much, and you will certainly not do your best work.

DISTRACTIONS

Earlier, it was noted that maintaining a relationship takes energy and focus, whether with your friend, significant other, parent, or even just a co-worker. This is also true of your relationships with your teachers, and with the course material, (to stretch the metaphor a bit). If, mentally, you are only half- or one-quarter present during classes, during study time, or while taking tests, do not expect your teacher/student relationships to thrive and grow. On any given day, and at any given moment, there are many things competing for our attention; Facebook, texting, lunch, and even sleeping. However, by keeping your focus on the subject at hand, you will learn more deeply, process information in more complex ways, and ultimately, perform better on tests (both oral & written).

This, by the way, is another reason to sit toward the front of the room. Fewer people and fewer devices will be part of your field of vision, so you will be less likely to be distracted. As you must know by now, learning often requires focused attention on a challenging topic, so by giving yourself all the advantages possible, and by sitting where the majority of your visual field is filled by the teacher, their Power Point, and/or Smart Board examples, you will be setting yourself up for success, and to be perceived in a positive light by your teachers.

RADICAL IDEA ALERT!

This is probably the single most radical topic in the entire book–the one idea that will stand out as completely odd. Here it is: **turn off your phone.** *No, I don't mean switch it to vibrate—which only distracts you a little—or switch it to silent mode and then keep it on your leg where you can see it. I mean actually* **turn it off.**

Now I can you hear you saying, "Chris, what if somebody calls or texts me, and I miss it? What then?" Well, to be blunt ... so what? They can leave a message, or a text, and you can get back to them later.

Sounds radical, doesn't it? Put 100% of your attention on your class for its duration. Unless you're a doctor-on-call or a volunteer fireman, you don't need to be continually available to your friends and family.

And as long as I'm promoting dangerous ideas here, I'm going to suggest another one: you should also turn off your phone when you're studying, and while you're sleeping. You may find yourself more relaxed, sleeping better, and performing better in school. Try it for a few days. It's just so crazy ...

BETTER GRADES

As it turns out, much of your school day is mental work. Studying, discussing, and reading, will comprise the bulk of your education. However, your choices – even as simple as choosing where to sit in a classroom – will affect your attention, focus, and ability to study. As an adult, you will make these choices for yourself, all the time. Start now and it will get easier and easier until it becomes your natural condition.

BEHAVE LIKE A GREAT STUDENT

Implementing everything we've been exploring here will not make you a great student. You still have to do the work, read the material, and get to class. But *acting* like a great student in class—with good posture, engaged eye contact, appropriate dress, and maximized seating position—will not only affect your teacher's perception of you, it will also affect how you feel about yourself. Put simply, modeling behaviors on the outside will influence how you feel on the inside, so "act" like a great student and you will be on your way to being one.

PERSONAL POV

OK, now it's time to share some of my own experiences.

I enjoyed college. It was a time of great learning, meeting new people, and having fun. I think part of my success was my enthusiasm, but also that I made some very deliberate choices about how I was going to "go" to college: I went to every class, sat near the front, resolved I would not quit in the middle of the semester, and occasionally took classes just for the fun of it. These choices made a huge difference in my college career, and with my GPA.

It turns out, my favorite class was a seminar in philosophy. I was a morning person in those days, so the 8am start time suited me perfectly. Plus, I have always loved to argue ...er, *have discussions*, which is what the class was all about.

There were twelve in the class, and we would all sit around a large conference table. The format of the class had us discuss an assigned reading in a free-form conversation, while the professor asked questions and gently guided the dialogue. The discussion could, and did, go just about anywhere. It was a blast.

A big problem with the class, though, was that it was nearly impossible to guess what would be on tests and quizzes. In fact, the first quiz was a shock for nearly everybody. Nobody scored as well as they had expected to, and everybody complained that the questions were impossible to anticipate, which made studying for a test very difficult. Since you're probably wondering, I got a B- on that first quiz. I was a straight-A student, and I intended to stay that way, so a B- was unacceptable. I was determined to find a way to better prepare for the quizzes.

Now, back in the early 1980's, it was common for professors to smoke in classrooms. By the third week of class I began to notice a curious pattern. At some point during our discussions, the professor's cigarette ash would get longer and longer. Why? He was taking more frequent drags on the cigarette and forgetting to tap off the ash. What the professor was demonstrating was an increase in pacifying behaviors. His excitement level (or what psychologists more accurately refer to as "arousal" level) was increasing, and he was using smoking to calm himself.

I reasoned that what he was excited about in our conversations was likely to be on the tests and quizzes. So I took extra-detailed notes at those moments, and I highlighted that information for extra study. It turned out I was right. The topics that the students discussed during his 'pacifying' moments were almost always the topics that appeared on the exams. As a result, I lifted my grade back up to the A that I wanted, and believed I could achieve.

Every professor has a 'tell' that will indicate what class material he or she finds particularly exciting or appealing. However, it's not always the case that this material will form the basis of the grading system, but it is usually the case that referencing this material during class discussions, or in papers, will help convince that professor that you have a strong mastery of the subject.

IX. LYING

This section was destined to be the most popular. After all, everyone wants to know the truth, and who to trust. While many areas of body language can be a lot of fun to study, this topic – lying - is much more serious.

The GOOD news:

We are all driven by our emotions. When we lie, the two sides of our brain come into conflict, which, in turn, causes *us*, as emotional beings, to experience conflict. In most cases, this conflict will be reflected in our physical lives; we will leak nonverbal cues like crazy. Sorting them out, and then analyzing them, can be an enormous challenge.

Some of the (possible) signs of lying:

- Face touching (particularly nose and mouth.)
- Hands covering mouth.
- Micro expressions.
- Looking away or failure to maintain eye contact.
- Verbal tics (uh, oh, ah) which are essentially time fillers while their brain makes up a story.

The BAD news:

No single action can tell you if a person is lying or telling the truth. Even clusters of behavior can only *help* you get a better read on a person's veracity—they are not definitive. The best

153

you can hope for is a feeling; does this person *seem* reliable; do I trust them *now?*

POLYGRAPHS, AND THEIR UNRELIABILITY

A polygraph is a machine that senses biological reactions and records them on a sheet of paper. It's also known as a "lie detector," but this name is not accurate. In fact, it's so inaccurate that polygraph results are not admissible in most court cases. Detecting lies is a real skill, and is more of an art than a science.

In my experience, the single most telling factor that can help you determine if someone is lying is not non-verbal at all ... it's their history. Have they lied before? Do they make a habit of lying? Have they lied to YOU before? I've found that people behave consistently; liars often lie, truth-tellers usually tell the truth. Most of them time.

POKER

Poker is currently one of the most popular games in the US, and here's a big secret: it's not just about rules and percentages. A winning poker strategy relies on reading the other people at the table, and learning their "tells." Watching their non-verbal cues will give an expert player valuable information. By careful observation of each player – how they react to cards being played, how they bet, and how they react to other players – an expert can predict how a person will react in the future. *"Mastery of poker is mastery of people."* And much of that is observation of non-verbal cues.

A master poker player will keep an eye out for sudden behavior changes. For example, Dave always bets big when he gets a pair of face cards. In much the same way, you should watch for changes in your target's behavior as well. People often act differently when telling a lie compared to when they are telling the truth.

TELLS

Definition: *A "tell" is a term used in Poker for an action or behavior that indicates the value of a player's hand.*

This behavior is so consistent, that it indicates to other players what cards he's holding, or at least, strength or weakness of his hand. Tells may also include ring-twisting, coughing, micro expressions, etc.

See the films *Maverick* or *Rounders* for good dramatizations of this.

Liars are usually caught through a series of observations – but not by observing just one twitch or unconscious movement. It takes time. Consistently spotting a liar is tough; even for the skilled, and the success rate is normally less than 50%.

After reviewing this book, and learning what is taught within, you will have some very powerful knowledge; use them only for good – never for evil.

CREATING A BASELINE

When studying body language, especially when trying to catch liars, it's useful to establish a baseline – or normal – set of behaviors. This is much the same as the idea of "context" discussed in previous chapters.

What does the person do in everyday life when he or she is telling the truth? When this behavior is established, you are now able to spot changes when (or if) he or she lies.

BECOME A HUMAN LIE DETECTOR

I outlined this experiment briefly in the chapter entitled, "Establishing a Baseline." Here is another version that I use in my live program, *Student Body Language*.

I split the audience up into pairs and I tell them that they will now have the chance to become human lie detectors. I explain that each will ask the other person three questions. When asked, they are each to respond truthfully to two of the questions, but they must lie when responding to the third. Additionally, they may choose to which question they will lie, and they are not to reveal which one they've chosen. The challenge is for the questioner to figure out which of the responder's answers are truthful, and which is the lie.

It's quite easy. Try this on a friend. Explain the rules, and then ask these three questions.

1) Where did you last go on vacation?

2) What is the name of your first girlfriend or boyfriend?

3) What kind of car was your very first car?

You don't have to use these questions specifically, but be sure to use questions that can't be answered with an easy "yes" or "no." They must require a longer answer and require some thought.

How do you tell which answer is the lie? Just watch their eyes. Out of three responses, the eyes will shift in the same direction for two, but will shift differently on the third. The answer accompanying the odd direction marks the lie.

In the past, I've discussed the myth concerning the direction a person's eyes shift when telling a lie; in short, it really doesn't matter in what direction they shift. With some people, they'll go right when they tell the truth, and with others they'll go left, and with others still, they may rotate, go up, etc. What you're looking for is not the direction in which they shift, but the fact that one out of the three times is different than the others.

You may have already guessed that I have an ulterior motive for teaching this game. I want everyone attending my programs—and you, the reader as well—to understand that

157

everybody has a different "normal" when it comes to their body language. Some people are naturally calm and relaxed, and some are naturally energetic. Some people move smoothly and elegantly, while others move with quick, choppy actions. The most revealing information comes when people depart from their norm. So start paying attention to how people behave from the moment you meet them. Try to determine what their 'normal' behavior is. Then, as you watch them over time, they'll be that much easier to read.

We do this baselining unconsciously; this is why, when we see someone on the street acting "weird," we know what "weird" is. They are acting differently than how we expect them to act. It's odd, and a little frightening, to get an unbidden message from your brain saying, "Watch out for that guy over there – they are acting out of the ordinary. Might be risky," when we didn't know we were paying attention.

This subconscious baselining is also the reason you can immediately tell when a friend is feeling down or having a bad day ... their baseline has changed. Perhaps John is usually a fast walker, with confident posture, and he zips right over to his usual table in the cafeteria. But today you see him meander, with his head down, to a corner booth; something is obviously different. His 'normal" has changed, and this behavior change most likely reflects his emotional state.

There is a broad range of what's normal – different people behave differently. There are also great differences in what is accepted behavior across cultures, generations, genders, and personalities. Baselining, however, is most useful when applied to one person at a time.

Remember, lying causes emotional upset in a person – it is a much more complex mental activity than telling the truth. Instead of just remembering and speaking (very instinctual), the speaker now has to make up a believable story, often on the spot, present it, and then monitor their own cues to "look normal." This often results in a large change in their nonverbals.

Keep in mind that even the best readers of nonverbal cues (police detectives, judges, Moms) can only *guess* at the truthfulness of a speaker, and their accuracy is usually somewhere in the 50% range. Using body language techniques *improves* your chances of catching a liar, but it does not *guarantee* results.

HOW TO STOP LOOKING LIKE A LIAR

You may never need to interrogate a criminal, or question someone to locate a missing million-dollar diamond, but the one thing you can definitely learn from this chapter is how to **not** look like a liar when you're telling the truth, and how to avoid situations where your actions and your body language are telling two different stories. After all, if you send mixed signals, people looking and listening to you won't know which story to believe; the one you're telling, or the one their subconscious is picking up. And your communication with this person will become tenuous.

Confusion often arises when listeners interpret a speaker's nervous behavior as "lying" behavior. A highly-trained observer can tell the difference, but a casual one may find it hard to differentiate; the two behaviors often overlap. Some people are just not used to speaking in public, or they get uncomfortable in social situations, thus, they appear uncomfortable and awkward. The way for you to avoid confusing *your* listeners is to reduce your levels of stress and anxiety with techniques like breathing, rehearsal, and visualization. This way, you won't appear uncomfortable or awkward … and have your behavior misinterpreted.

However, keep in mind that some of these "pacifying" behaviors are well known and may make people suspicious of you. There exists a stereotype of the shifty-eyed, sweaty, nervous individual (usually a guy), who is later found to be lying.

When communicating, remember that everyone knows a little bit about body language, but what they know is usually limited to some (real or imagined)"lying" cues, e.g. open and closed body language, the whole nose scratching thing, etc.

Furthermore, effective and clear communication is often difficult for speakers from one region of the country to appear credible to listeners from another region, or from one country to the next, etc. The expected "normal" behavior is very different, and subsequently, one or the other feels "off."

Because of all this, determining baseline body language, and then observing changes in that body language, remains the most effective and successful way to cut through the clutter of personal idiosyncrasies & regionalisms, and to make informed decisions about the veracity of a speaker.

IX. THE BODY LANGUAGE OF RAPPORT

Have you ever met somebody for the first time, and felt that you simply "aligned" with them? That you were, "on the same frequency," or you just "clicked?"

These words and phrases are all euphemisms for something called … rapport.

Rapport: being in synch with another person; defining similar interests and developing common ground, all working toward creating a 'like' in another person.

One of the most interesting aspects of, and practical uses for, body language is the role it can play when developing rapport with other people.

It is especially useful when forming *new* relationships, or *deepening* existing ones. At this point in the book, it shouldn't surprise you to learn that there are nonverbal techniques that, when used properly, can accelerate the process.

Now, there are books out there that claim that they can teach you how to create "instant rapport" in 60 seconds or less. This is simply not true, and luckily, most people are not naïve enough to believe that if two people sit in the same manner, or do something equally simplistic, they will suddenly become best buddies for life. It just doesn't happen that quickly.

However, this chapter will explore nonverbal tools and techniques that support the *development* of warm and emotionally rich relationships. These techniques will be ESPECIALLY helpful to those whose personality is often perceived as "cold" or "off-putting."

One of my go-to techniques when interacting with others is deep intellectual discussion. I like hearing about, and discussing, interesting ideas, subjects in the news, and books. But I realize that in many situations, people would rather discuss sports, their kids, or their favorite hobby – possibly fly fishing or unicycle juggling.

If my goal is to build rapport with them, I will need to put my favorite subjects aside for a while and work to discover some commonalities. Also, this is not the time to argue with people about their beliefs. This will definitely not help you build a warm and trusting friendship. Constructive argumentation only develops between two people who already respect one another, or at least believes that the other person's opinions are worthy of consideration.

When it comes right down to it, the key to building rapport is a combination of 1) quality time spent with another person, and 2) a focus on them. Once again we find that open body language, active listening, good eye contact, and providing feedback, are used to help create better communication. The word "rapport" comes from the French verb *"rapporter,"* which means, literally, "to carry something back." It's all about give-and-take.

By the way, there is nothing dishonest about using the techniques of rapport; you are merely putting your focus and energy on another person to determine what you have in common, and to see if you will get along. Conversation is certainly part of building rapport, and you will need to spend time finding out more about each other, discussing common likes and dislikes, and just being in close physical proximity.

What follows are several areas to explore when attempting to build rapport.

ONE-ON-ONE

Building rapport is something best done with one person at a time. It takes time, focus, the gentle give-and-take of conversation, and the enjoyment of silences. I have found that most true relationships are built this way, rather than in large groups.

Have you ever noticed that when you are with your closest, dearest friend, you can often sit for extended periods of time without saying anything? You simply enjoy and appreciate their company? That's TRUE rapport. And that takes a great deal of time and effort (and serendipity) to develop.

NOTE: It is possible to build rapport with several people at once, but I'll leave that to a future book because it's a fairly advanced skill.

FACE-TO-FACE

When interacting and speaking with another person, it's best to sit face-to-face, head on, because creating rapport is much easier when you can see and hear each other well.

SETTING

While you might be able to build rapport at a baseball game (it is a shared activity), or in a busy restaurant (another shared activity, especially if it's a new, untried restaurant), the distractions inherent in places like this may work against you. When you seek to do some serious rapport-building, try and find a place that is quiet and relatively free from outside activity. It doesn't have to be the library, but it's best to avoid trying to build rapport in a mosh pit.

TIME

As already discussed, developing a relationship requires an initial commitment of time. If you wish to maintain a strong rapport over time, then you'll need to develop an on-going commitment of time throughout the relationship. This entails routinely devoting mindshare and focus on the other person; listening to them, and attending to their needs. In rapport building, this means setting aside time in your life *regularly,* away from everything else. There is no way around this.

ENERGY

One of the ways we feel attuned to another person is the discovery that they are like us. On a very basic level, this means that they match, at least superficially, our own energy level. So, when using this type of "mirroring" in rapport building, you must first define the other person's energy level. Is it subdued and quiet? Agitated and jumpy? Or perhaps animated and expressive? When identified, adjust your energy level to more closely match or augment theirs. Adjusting your physical and vocal energy to compliment theirs validates them—it gives them permission to act naturally, and subsequently, to be comfortable. It says, nonverbally, *"Hey, I'm here with you. I'm like you. Feel free to be you."*

FEEDBACK

People are always on the lookout for feedback. It enables them to know that they're being heard and understood. Appropriate signals like nodding for agreement, and uttering things like "yes' and "OK" occasionally are effective. The Japanese culture, especially, regards this as a natural, and almost mandatory, part of any sort of polite interaction.

RESPECT

Being respectful of another person boils down to two things:

1)   **Listening to their ideas:** While you don't have to agree with *everything* they say, you should at least listen and try to understand why they believe what they believe, or why they feel the way they feel.

2)   **The expectation of privacy:** One way to quickly break someone's trust is to broadcast their secrets to the world. When in doubt, ask their permission, or don't the share the information at all.

MEN & RAPPORT

Women routinely get together to chat and "catch-up," and are generally more practiced at building rapport. Men do not generally take this tack, but they have their own ways of connecting. As a rule, men choose to get together under the pretext of a shared activity, e.g. working on a project, fixing a computer, watching a game, etc. The dynamics of these interactions are generally very different than those of women (and a painful number of books have been devoted to the subject), but the goal is the same – building a relationship through sharing information and/or a shared experience.

MIRRORING

One of the key concepts in creating rapport with another person is mirroring their behavior, including matching their stance, their gestures, their overall energy level, and their voice. You are *literally* getting in synch with them. Clearly, you must do this in subtle ways—this is not an episode of I Love Lucy—but it helps create synchronicity when you adjust yourself to their vocal level, their physical level (sitting or standing), and their emotional level (calm, agitated, etc.). NOTE: In a real-world situation, where another person is physically, mentally, and/or emotionally upset, it may not be a good idea to "mirror" their volatility. You can, however, make allowances for their mental, emotional, and physical state and adjust your own vocal rhythm, posture, and overall energy to be *sympathetic* to theirs. As they say on Project Runway, you don't want to be too "matchy-matchy."

During everyday interactions, mirroring must remain very subtle. You shouldn't instantly copy everything someone does. If you did, your behavior would look very weird. It's much more nuanced than that—it's understanding and augmenting their style of conversation and their physical life. In short, if they are excited, you can reflect and enhance this excitement; if they are becoming quiet, you can tune in to it. These adjustments will let the other person know that you're present with them, and that you're committed to communicating and understanding them.

Think of mirroring as complimenting a person's *overall style*, and not simply mimicking them gesture for gesture.

EYE CONTACT

Once again, we find that *visually* focusing on another person is helpful in creating rapport. Looking at a person generally means that you're paying attention to them and their emotional state. Parents routinely direct their children to, "Look at Mr. So-and-so when you talk to them," or, "Look at me when I'm talking to you." Engaging a speaker visually demonstrates respect, and forces the "looker" to pay better attention to the "lookee."

Rapport *can* be created sitting side-by-side in a car, or over the phone, but it's much easier to do when facing the other person. People tend to open up more if they have visual confirmation that you're listening.

QUID PRO QUO

One aspect of friendship is doing favors for one another without looking for anything material in return. This "lack of quid pro quo" is also an effective tactic when creating rapport. It doesn't have to entail huge gifts or performing time-consuming tasks like watching her dog for a week. It could merely be helping pick something out, or finding an appropriate book at the library. While most adults are fully independent, they still like receiving small gifts, or having small favors done for them. This kind of help is a wonderful way to start any relationship.

USING THEIR NAME

I mention this in passing because using someone's name in a conversation is one of the most popular, and least successful, techniques in creating rapport. This is based on the observation that we all like to be recognized, and that we all like hearing our own name. However, this technique has been almost exclusively adopted by politicians and salespeople, and they routinely do it poorly. Mentioning someone's name once or twice during a conversation is fine, but it's very easy to overdo it. It can go from being "nice," to being "insincere," to "creepy," rather quickly. Simply repeating someone's name is not a magic spell that will cause a person to open their wallets or instantly give you their phone number.

Whenever I see an interview with a politician, and the politician uses the interviewer's name six to eight times in a matter of minutes, I get very suspicious. It makes me think that the politician is covering something up.

GIVE-AND-TAKE

Conversations, friendships, and rapport building requires a give-and-take. Remember the French derivation? Sometimes you listen, sometimes you talk. We all live inside our heads, and we all love certain things, especially hearing ourselves talk. After all, most of us find ourselves pretty interesting. But if you want to build rapport, you need to get out of your head and allow your conversation partner to speak and to choose the direction of the conversation. It takes practice to maintain this kind of balance in a conversation—especially for alpha personalities, or for very time-focused people, and for some men. (I include myself in this last group.)

Now, this does not mean that you should lean back, cross your arms, and bide your time while the other person talks, impatiently waiting for your turn to say something fascinating. This behavior stops you from being an active participant in the conversation, and casts you as a bench-warmer impatiently waiting to get in the game and shine. Perfect for sports, lousy for conversations. Like it or not, when you behave like this, you *will* communicate this attitude through your body language. You need to remain engaged, listening, and focused. Yes, this takes energy and time.

An effective regimen is something we'll call, "power listening." It means *truly* paying attention to other people in your life, and using certain techniques to actually hear what they're saying.

I'm so fascinated by this topic that I've written a presentation and blog on it. If you're interested look it up in my webpage christophercartermentalist.com.

An example of rapport building

Most people think that in order to "get the girls," you have be a great looking guy. This isn't the case. A friend of mine in college always seemed to attract women, in spite of his being—at best—an average looking guy. In fact, his social success went well beyond his attractiveness to the opposite sex. He was the sort of person to whom people just seemed to gravitate - both men and women.

What was his secret? I'm sure he had many, but the biggest one was his instinctive mastery of nonverbal communication. Being very shy at the time, I was envious of his ease in social situations, and since I had a strong interest in body language, I decided to study him.

*The most striking thing I noticed was that every time he started to talk to someone, he would mirror them. Not only would he adjust his posture and movement to more closely match theirs, he would also adjust to their personal rhythms. If they were energetic, **he** would become more energetic. If their movements were slower, **he** would slow down.*

However, his changes were never abrupt. He would adapt gradually and naturally. If you weren't specifically looking for it, it would never occur to you that his behavior had changed.

> *I have no reason to believe that my friend was aware of what he was doing. It came to him naturally. Far from making him seem insincere, his mirroring caused his conversation partner to feel as if they were the most important person in the world.*

FAKING IT

Let's explore how to fake rapport.

Yes, this is not a very noble aspiration, but it is useful when trying to take control of a difficult or stressful situation.

Very often, when we find ourselves in a challenging situation, we try to gain control of it through the use of anger, or by leveraging our status. This is the exact opposite of building rapport.

When creating rapport, your body is neutral and relaxed, your voice is friendly, and you spend more time listening than talking. The rapport you build may not be deep, or truly meaningful, but it may finesse a difficult situation and help you achieve a desired goal

> *I travel quite a bit for business, so often I need a bit of help, or a favor, from a clerk. Repeatedly, I have found that the best approach is to not get angry or berate them, but simply to make a friendly request. I find that when I do this, people are more interested in helping me. This is creating rapport at its most basic level. People who calmly and politely* request *things, rather than* demand *them, often get what they need, and sometimes, they gain a friend along the way.*

Now, one of the problems with rapport-building techniques is that they are often part of low-quality salesmanship training events, or are featured in cheesy dating videos that you can buy on TV after midnight for $29.95. The difference is that when building *honest* rapport, you're *truly* trying to connect with the other person, you *truly* listen, and you *truly* care about what they have to say. You are not just selling them carpeting or trying to get your hotel room upgraded.

In short, the difference is … honesty. If your only goal is to fool someone into thinking that you like them, then yes, the "rapport" you build may work, but only for short time. If your goal is to create strong, *long-term* relationship—you'll have better success.

> *To experience the strength of these techniques, I suggest the following experiment: The next time you meet somebody, in addition to listening to them, try to mirror their energy, emotional state, and physicality, and note how it affects their interest in you, and your subsequent connection.*

AN ASIDE ON TRIBES

As much as we like to think we're multicultural, inclusive, and universal, we, as a society, tend to associate with people who are most like us. We become members of a tribe (to use an anthropological term). We may be a member of several different types of tribes at once, but underneath, they will most likely share common traits, goals, ambitions, etc. To prove this to yourself, take a closer look at the groups in which you are a member, e.g. your friends, your clubs, your church, even your entire school; at their root, they're probably a fairly homogeneous bunch. They are a "tribe." This, however, isn't a bad thing—in fact, it's an integral part of our survival instinct. Loners don't do well in the wilderness … or in the wilds of a college campus.

In order to grow as a person, it's also important that we venture outside of our tribe from time to time. This may take some serious effort, because it's easier to connect with like-minded people. To build rapport with people who *do not* share any of our life experience is a lot of work.

When you make the effort to meet and connect with people from vastly different backgrounds, experience, and perspectives, you will not only get better at building rapport, you will also become a more perceptive human being.

THE LIMITATIONS OF RAPPORT

The simple truth is – you may attempt to build rapport with someone, and it simply doesn't work. You just don't click, no matter how hard you try. You can certainly *improve* that relationship, or at least keep it from being a *negative* one, but that may be it. Ah well, c'est la vie. The fact is … not everyone is going to like you, and frankly, *you* are not going to like everyone. This is okay. Most people have a fairly small group of close friends, and don't feel the need for a whole lot more.

EMPATHY

Empathy, or the ability to sense what another person is feeling, is certainly an important part of rapport. When you understand what somebody else is going through, or where their thoughts and feelings are coming from, it's easier to relate to them and build rapport. Developing empathy takes time and sensitivity to reading cues. For instance, the difference between depression and fatigue is subtle, but important. In fact, a lack of empathy is one of the hallmarks of sociopathic behavior.

What we are truly talking about here is the ability to relate to someone else's situation, and sublimate our own needs for the moment. This is common among couples. One partner gets their work done and is excited to go out, and the other partner is ready to kick up their feet and watch a movie. Two different people, with two different expectations, and two different energy levels. Clearly, they will have to work out a compromise, or one will need to give in to what the other wants. "Empathy" on one, or both, their parts makes this possible. There's that give-and-take again.

If someone is brave enough, and trusts you enough, to drop their day-to-day emotional mask in front of you, pay special attention. It often means that they're taking a risk and recognizing the possibility that you're a worthwhile person to know.

Finally, rapport building is likely one of the most important, and hardest, skills to acquire in the nonverbal toolbox. This is especially true if you don't have a great deal of experience in social settings. On the other hand, keep in mind that like most every other technique detailed in this book, you may have been using it for years, but you simply weren't conscious of it.

Three easy exercises for building your rapport skills:

1.   The next time you're chatting with one of your friends, instead of talking about yourself, shift the conversation to focus on them. Ask what she has been up to, and what her plans are. This is actually a little difficult for most people; after all, our mental script is normally, "Me, me, me." Try to actively adjust your behavior and, for at least a few minutes, focus on and listen to them, and practice your nonverbals of agreement; yeses, nodding etc.

2.   In order to strengthen your "out-going" muscles, try, for one full day, smiling at every person you see. Yes, you will feel like a dope, but it will also be fun. When meeting new people, try to remember more than their names—try to discover something fascinating about them. This will make you more inquisitive (which is them-focused), and will help you connect more strongly with them in the future (thus building more rapport).

3.   This will be either the easiest, or the hardest, exercise of the three. For a week, target one person per day to whom you will pay a genuine compliment, emphasis on the word "genuine." Verbalize something you find interesting or fascinating about them. Do this without expectation of reward or reciprocity, and see what happens. (Of course, you'll find yourself looking for interesting people to talk to, and that is kind of the point, yes?)

*A friend of mine's Father once said to him, **"If you want to do someone a favor, let them do one for you."** I've found this to be true time and time again. Very often, we shy away from letting people impact our lives. It's a symptom of our individualistic society and up-bringing. This is most apparent when we push back against people who want to do something for us. For example, someone says to us, "Hey, let me get that for you …," or "Coffee's on me," we often respond with, "No, no, I'm fine – I got it …" or "Oh no, I couldn't possibly let you pay …"*

Believe it or not, in many cases, you are insulting that person. You are subtly saying that you do not wish to be beholden to them. Extreme? Yes, but the subliminal implication is there. When someone does you a favor, they are, at the very least, trying to be polite, or, at best, they are telling you that you matter to them, and that they wish to have a better, deeper relationship with you.

Favors, as we've discussed, are rapport builders, and by rejecting someone's favors, you are, in essence, saying that you do not wish to have any rapport with them. Of course, exceptions are made for stalkers, psychopaths, etc. or people who pathologically pick up checks, buy inappropriately expensive gifts, etc.

Rapport building is a two-way street, and you must learn to identify when others are trying to build it with you. Nonverbal cues are subtle, covert actions that reveal how a person is feeling about you. Favors are not-so-subtle, overt cues that reveal how they feel about you. Don't be clueless.

The next time someone offers to do you a favor, graciously smile and say, "Thank You. I appreciate that." Your relationship with that person will deepen, and your rapport with that person will grow … guaranteed.

XI. FIRST IMPRESSIONS

Meeting the parents, job interviews, and other important moments in your life people forget how crucial, and how long-lasting, first impressions are.

First impressions consist almost entirely of nonverbal cues, and occur within fractions of a second. Once the impression is formed, it is carved in stone, and it is very difficult to change.

When people meet you for the first time, they make some very important decisions immediately:

1)   If they like you
2)   If they trust you
3)   If you have valid authority

Since we tend to help people we like and trust, or follow those we feel have credible authority, first impressions are about more than getting invited to a party.

JOB INTERVIEWS

Inevitably, you will be invited to an important meeting with a course advisor, to a job interview, or to an initial introduction to your significant other's parents. Clearly, these encounters could make a huge difference in your future.

All first-impression situations have some very specific rules and your nonverbal communication plays a key role. What follows are several important areas that need attention.

DRESS, TIME AND FORMAL BEHAVIORS

In most cases, you will enter *their* space (office, business, or home) as a visitor. You may be expected to "ask for permission" to enter, either in the form of an appointment, through an intermediary, or simply by knocking at the front door and waiting to be asked in.

Some people are more possessive of their personal space than others are. High-status individuals reinforce their position by controlling the environment around them. An effective way to appear more dominant is to "take over" somebody else's personal space. (Think of the boss who comes in and sits on an employee's desk.) If you were to try and take over the space of someone who is not very high in status, you may get away with it. But if you tried that with someone with higher status, you will be setting yourself up for a fall. It is a strategy recommended for a time when someone is trying to intimidate you, and should only to be used as a defensive tactic. Otherwise, it should be avoided.

PHYSICALITY

The first thing we do when meeting someone, even before shaking hands, is make eye contact and smile. These two actions have the potential to convey warmth, friendliness, and honesty.

It may seem like eye contact is something that can't possibly be done incorrectly, but in fact, there is a right way and a wrong way. Imagine that there's a triangle formed between the eyes that goes down to the bottom of the nose. We'll call this triangle the "lower gaze" zone. Now imagine a triangle that links their eyes and the forehead. We'll call this the "upper gaze" zone. Making eye contact in the "lower gaze zone" conveys warmth and friendliness, while making eye contact in the "upper gaze" zone is perceived as intimidating or aloof.

As for smiles, there are two kinds: the social (or artificial) smile, and the genuine (or Duchesne) smile. The social smile is one we paste onto our faces even though we don't really feel it. The genuine smile is an honest expression of happiness and joy. The difference is in the eyes. Genuine smiles not only involve the mouth, but also activate the muscles around the eyes, so that your eyes crinkle as you smile. False smiles only activate the muscles around the mouth. Infants can tell the difference between a genuine and a false smile almost from the moment of birth. Adults may not be consciously aware of it, but they will "feel" the difference, and they will be more attracted to the genuine smile. *They'll also judge the person who gives a genuine smile to be more trustworthy.*

This will sound odd, but it's actually possible to fake a genuine smile. If you raise your eyebrows, or "flash" them just a little as you start to smile, your smile will spread to your entire face.

The world of business has many formal expectations, more than we experience in everyday school life. The next sections will explore several of these in more detail.

DRESS & FASHION

Depending on the position and industry, you may be expected to dress up. In general, this entails wearing business attire, meaning dress shoes and a tie for the men. Women have a few more choices, but are expected to stick to classic and conservative outfits. Pay attention to being well groomed, neat, and clean as well.

BEING ON TIME

When you are aiming to make a good, or great, first impression, people will – and they cannot help this – judge you by your actions and choices. Being on time shows respect, and with regards to a job or internship interview, it also shows THAT YOU CAN BE ON TIME!

Use of time varies heavily from culture to culture. In American culture, punctuality is a must, and as explored earlier in this book, time in Latin America is regarded much more casually. The important thing to understand is the expectation of your target audience. Also, arriving early is not necessarily better. If arriving early inconveniences the person with whom you are meeting, it may send a message that you are demanding or difficult to work with. Being on time will also reduce your stress level and help you look more composed.

THE ART OF THE HANDSHAKE

Within 30 seconds of meeting a person for the first time, they will decide two very important things about you. They will decide whether they like you, and whether they trust you. The scary part is that they will not make these decisions consciously. These decisions will be based on intuition, or "gut" instinct, and they will be communicated primarily by your body language. A major influence on this gut feeling is your handshake.

There are three basic styles of handshakes:

1.   **The classic grip:** Your hand is perpendicular to the floor and facing the other person's hand.

2.   **The palm-down grip:** Your hand is angled so that your palm faces somewhat toward the floor, and you grasp the other person's hand from above;

3.   **Palm-up grip:** Your palm faces more toward the sky, and you grasp the person's hand from below.

Within each of these styles is room for many variations. For example, you may encounter somebody shaking your hand with a two-handed variation of the palm-down grip: their right hand grasps from above, while their left hand grasps from below. I sometimes call this version the "Used Car Salesman's Grip." You'll find it used in situations where people are trying to dominate you, or give you a "hard-sell."

The palm-up equivalent of this—in which your right hand grasps from below while your left hand grasps from above—is one you will often see used to console people who are stricken with grief. I'll get into the meanings of these various styles in a moment, but for now, the important thing to remember is that each variation creates a different impression in the mind of the person you are greeting.

I doubt anybody knows for certain how the handshake evolved as a form of greeting. It probably had something to do with demonstrating that you were not carrying a weapon and posed no threat. I can say for sure, however, that the handshake provides a perfect opportunity to size the other person up. It gives you an immediate sense of their confidence, strength, whether they seem friendly or threatening, and even whether they will be difficult to deal with, or be a pushover.

In general, you will create your best impression if you demonstrate that you are confident and approachable. You will be perceived as neither overly dominant, nor overly submissive. To create this impression, the key tactic to be aware of when shaking hands is the angle of your hand and the strength of your grip.

The palm-down grip is very dominating. You are showing you want to be "on top." It becomes even more so in its two-handed form. The only time you would want to use this is if you're being greeted by somebody who is clearly trying to dominate you. In this case, your handshake lets them know that you can't be easily pushed around.

The palm up grip is submissive. There are situations where it can be calming, for example when consoling somebody, but I can think of very few other situations where its use would be desirable. In most cases, it will stand as an open invitation to victimize you.

The classic grip is the most neutral, and the one that conveys the most openness. With this grip, you are perceived as an equal, which contributes to you being regarded as likeable.

The ideal strength of your grip depends upon whose hand you're shaking. My advice is to apply pressure equal to that from the other person. Also, take stock of your natural strength. If you are very strong, you may want to get into the habit of using a lighter grip. If you are very weak, it may be a good idea to do some grip exercises to build up your power.

When it comes to creating a positive impression, it's usually the body language cues we think about *the least* that have the strongest impact. This is particularly true of the handshake. Its power stems from the fact that it's one of the first cues we emit when meeting a person, and research shows that initial impressions last the longest. In fact, they're so powerful that they become the benchmark by which all your future behavior is judged. So spend some time thinking about your own handshake, and ask yourself, "Does it create the positive impression I want? "Does it make me appear too dominant, or too submissive?" A little practice is all it takes to create a positive first impression every time.

Am I really suggesting here that you practice a firm, warm handshake? Yes. Like any other behavior, it works better when you are used to it. You probably don't shake hands with your mom or your friends, yet it is an essential part of operating in the world of business.

ADD A SMILE

When you shake hands and say hello, look the person in the eye and smile. It's a brief, but essential, ritual that says, "I'm ready to do business and am part of the tribe."

DON'T BULLY

A crushing handshake is a power play—it sets you up as a bully. It's a bad first impression. Think "firm." Also, think "gentler" with senior citizens and royalty. No fancy fist-bumps, or sixteen-step fancy-pants shakes, either; just the basic grip, one or two pumps, and release. Simple is best … truly.

LAST IMPRESSIONS

Last impressions are called the latency effect. Simply put, the way we remember somebody when we last saw him or her will have a disproportionate effect on what we think or feel about them the next time we see them. If we remember them doing something really clumsy or embarrassing the last time we saw them, that's the dominant impression that will be in our minds when we see them again.

This, by the way, is why we are so surprised when our favorite actor ages. We tend to remember them from their last movie, which may have been filmed ten years ago. Our mental image of them has not caught up with an actual, current image of them.

Auditory effects tend to have a more lasting effect than visual, though visuals will have a more lasting effect if they're particularly distinctive. If you wear a particularly flashy tie, you will be remembered, but not for your skills or friendly personality. In their minds, you'll be "the guy with the flashy tie." This suggests that it's important to keep your eyes on the prize, and not try to anchor something in someone's mind that is distracting.

Last impressions, or "departure rituals," could include shaking hands, hugging, kissing on the cheek, slapping on the ass, or fist bump. Choosing the appropriate way to make your departure will depend on culture, the person, your relationship with that person, and context. You wouldn't fist bump the person who just interviewed you for a job, unless perhaps you were interviewing for some very hip or trendy position. You wouldn't air kiss your friends after a rugby game.

Despite the fact that departure rituals should be appropriate to context, many people tend to stick with the strategies they know well, or with which they have become very comfortable. For example, people who like to hug will leave with a hug, even though they've had ample opportunity to notice that the person with whom they are talking is touch averse. It makes more sense to be sensitive to the needs of the other person and adapt to them.

Departure rituals should reinforce the positive messages you established when you first made contact. Specifically, your nonverbal cues should reinforce the perception that you're likable, confident, and trustworthy.

In show business, there's an adage that you must have a great opener and a fantastic closer, and it doesn't much matter what comes in between. It turns out that there's some good science to support this. Your first and last impressions are the most powerful, so finish strong. Think about the end of a meeting, date or interview and prepare to leave a positive lasting impression. When the meeting ends, stand up, shake hands with the person or people with whom you are meeting, say thank you, and make your exit.

Last Impressions are often **lasting impressions**, so choose your exit carefully, both in the statements you make, and the things your nonverbals say.

THE FAILURE OF TEXTING ...

... and other non-face-to-face communication.

Have you ever noticed how often a text or email gets misinterpreted? And then it takes five more to explain what you *really* meant?

This is due to the fact that a text is just words, with no surrounding information to communicate important context. Every time we have a face-to-face conversation, we hear and see much more than just the words—we see the speaker's emotional state, level of energy, facial expressions, vocal volume, word inflection and emphasis—and we get immediate feedback to see if our message is being understood. None of this is present when texting. Even emoticons and text-abbreviations—originally devised to help alleviate this situation—can be misinterpreted.

For example ... LOL? After you "laughing out loud" AT me, or WITH me?

A text is great for short, specific reminders such as "meet me at 8," but fails at communicating more complex issues.

There is an actor's exercise that tests how many different ways a line can be read. Each actor adds different emotions, stresses, character, and emphasis to a line to create a new feel and meaning. Try this yourself. How many different ways can you say the following lines:

- "Is that you?"
- "Come here right now."
- "Everything is ruined, going to the train station, destroy the creamery."

Without any surrounding information, each line can be interpreted in many different ways. Text messages are the same. How often has this happened to you; you get a text that makes no sense, until you realize who it's from?

In essence, all of the non-verbal information had been stripped out of the message, but then, when you learned who sent it—someone you know well—you can surround it and filter it through all sorts of context; your friend's specific point of view, the way he or she speaks, their sense-of-humor, etc. Then, as if by magic, communication occurs! This example paints a vivid picture of how hard it is to convey emotion, empathy, or emphasis when sending electronic forms of communication.

FLIRTING BY TEXT

When communicating by text, Twitter, Facebook, email, etc. remember that you are sending words without much, if any, context. They are, therefore, very easy to misinterpret. Save important conversations for a time when you can meet face-to-face, or at least speak on the telephone. Your communication and understanding will be much more successful.

Also, double-check to whom you are sending a text, especially flirty or suggestive ones; remember, your Mom's phone number is in your phone too.

THE DISTRACTION OF YOUR PHONE DEVICE

Once, I was people-watching while sitting in a food court in a mall. A young man and woman were talking, and it looked to me, after observing the guy's body language, that he had a romantic interest in the girl. As they spoke, the guy apparently received a notification of some sort on his smart phone. He picked it up to check it. The moment he did, the girl froze, and then leaned back from him. When he returned to the conversation, she crossed her arms and continued to close off her body to him from that point forward. Whatever romantic hopes the poor guy had were dashed by the simple act of picking up and checking his phone while she was talking. Imagine what might have happened if, instead of checking the phone, he had made a show of turning if off and putting it away.

How you use your phone in a social setting is an important choice. Constant texting, web-surfing, message-checking, and call-answering, displays a lack of respect for those present. It takes you out of the moment.

Perhaps everyone's greatest psychological need is to feel they're important to someone else. When you really listen to somebody, when you're clearly attentive to them, you're satisfying that need in them. Being inattentive tells the person they're not important to you.

The ultimate sign of respect – on a date or in a classroom – is have to have your phone off. The act of turning the phone off can be a powerful and useful ritual; a way of showing somebody that you have put aside all other interests to attend to them. I use it quite deliberately whenever I begin a business conversation or a personal conversation with somebody that I am meeting for the first time.

XIII. FAQS FOR REAL PEOPLE

I hope you have been enjoying this book, and as we near the end of our journey, I thought I would include some of the common questions I receive, along with answers you may find useful and helpful. Some of this information is covered in the book, but I find that a Quick Reference like this is helpful.

Q: What is nonverbal communication?

A Briefly, it is information that is relayed to another person without the use of words, or delivered while words are being spoken. It includes facial expressions, body movements, and the way we use things, like fashion and color.

Q: Is it unethical to use the nonverbal techniques detailed in this book?

A: Reading this book, and learning more about yourself, will certainly give you an advantage in life. However, these techniques are not a secret, and are easy to find. Many of them are based in common sense and simple observation. Some people are *naturally* skilled at reading body language, and require no training, but for the rest of us (myself included), we need some help to develop our body-language-reading skills. Finally, there's nothing dishonest about being self-aware, mindful, and working hard to communicate well with others.

Q: I'm fine with not looking like a model, but will learning to read body language help me be more interesting and attractive?

A: This is a loaded question. Body language cannot make you someone you are not, but it CAN help you accentuate who you are, and improve your communication skills. It can also help you better understand others. Body language can provide insight into what someone – perhaps the person in whom you're interested - is thinking and feeling, which will, in turn, help you adjust your behavior to be more "in synch" with them. Your connection with this person, subsequently, has a much better chance of evolving into something more. However, I guarantee that if you are not sensitive to what someone else is thinking or feeling, there will be NO CHANCE of a real relationship evolving. Therefore, understanding body language can help you be the best person you can be.

Q: Do I really need a firm handshake?

A: In short, yes, especially if you wish to make a good first impression. It is second only to your smile in the first-impression department.

Q: I attend a very large school, but often I feel alone. Is there anything you would suggest I do to meet more people?

A: I'm glad to be of help! One of the things to keep in mind, when looking to connect with other people, is to "pay attention." For example, when you are in the cafeteria, going to class, or attending a social event, be on the look-out for other people you find interesting, but who are also standing or sitting alone. If their body language says, "I'm new here, I'm shy, but I'm open to new experiences," that's a perfect person to meet. Go introduce yourself (that's a whole different book!). As you interact with them, monitor their body language to see if your approach is welcome. And of course, monitor your OWN body language to optimize the messages you're sending.

Q: Are you telling me that (when considering studying body language), I have to work on something new? I already have a job, a girlfriend, and a full class load.

A: Actually, body language can only be truly studied while interacting with other people in various situations. Therefore, the fact that you are already involved with people in different situations is a plus. Body language, on the whole, is fairly simple to understand and implement. Its application will pay off over your lifetime with better communication, unlike a class I took years ago called, "The Uke and You."

Q: But Chris, it feels unnatural to do some of these things.

A: Any new behavior requires time to feel natural. If you play a sport, adopting a new move or stance will feel "unnatural" at first because your mind and your body aren't familiar with it. Over time, and after your performance improves, you will wonder how you can have ever done it differently. The same is true of body language. And when it comes to applying your new skills, don't try to do everything at once. You will look furtive at best, and frantic at worst. The best approach is to adopt one or two new practices at a time, and see how they work for you. This may include smiling at more people, using more open body language, or, literally, standing up for yourself as we discussed in leadership chapter. Slow and steady wins the race.

Q: Can I use these techniques to get someone to fall in love with me?

A: No. Love is a complex psychological state. The best outcome you can achieve is to get people to notice you in a more positive fashion, to help you send consistent messages that you are warm and friendly, and to better understand how and what people are thinking and feeling. After that, when it comes to love, it's in the stars.

Q: Won't people know I'm doing this? It seems kind of obvious and little fake.

A: The answer is yes, sometimes they will. They'll notice that you've changed and that you're acting differently. That's fine, because one can only hope that they are *also* noticing that you're paying more attention and working hard to make your relationship work.

Q: What about me? I'm short, International, disabled, bigger, intellectual, older ... just overall a bit different. I feel awkward because I don't blend in with the rest of the group.

A: This is a great chance to use your uniqueness as an asset. All the things that make you, "YOU," help you to stand out and be noticed. Your job after that is to use inviting body language to meet new people and send positive signals.

Q: I don't have much time. What is the number one tip for a student wanting to improve her body language?

A: That's simple. One of the easiest, fastest, and most powerful techniques is simply this: smile. It lets people know that you're friendly, and normally causes others to smile back, and a smile is a great place to start any relationship.

XIV. STUDENT BODY LANGUAGE

REFERENCES & RESOURCES

Here are some of the books, places, people, and websites I sourced when researching this book. If you're interested in learning more, take a look for yourself.

- Shontell, Alyson (April 13, 2011) Business Insider: "If you look like this, you're destined for billions."

http://www.businessinsider.com/if-you-look-like-this-youre-destined-to-be-rich-2011-4?op=1

COLOR THEORY

- Johann Wolfgang Goethe -- Theory of Colours.

OLFACTICS

- Bering, Jesse (May 13, 2009) Scientific American Armpit Psychology: The science of body-order perception.
http://www.scientificamerican.com/article.cfm?id=armpit-psychology-body-odor

- Furlow, F. Bryant (March 1, 1996) Psychology Today: "The Smell of Love."
http://www.psychologytoday.com/articles/200910/the-smell-love

- Welsh, Jennifer (June 16, 2011) Live Science "Smell of success: scents affect thought, behaviors.

http://www.livescience.com/14635-impression-smell-thoughts-behavior-flowers.html

GENERAL BODY LANGUAGE

- Andersen, Peter A. (2004) The Complete Idiot's Guide to Body Language; Alpha Books.

- Navarro, Joe (2008) What Every Body is Saying; Harper Collins.

- Reiman, Tonya (2007) The Power of Body Language; Pocket Books - Simon & Schuster.

- Winter, Jessica, (8/14/2013) Slate Magazine; "The Kindly Brontosaurus."
http://www.slate.com/articles/life/culturebox/2013/08/the_kindly_brontosaurus_the_amazing_prehistoric_posture_that_will_get_you.html

DATING

- Reiman, Tonya (2012) The Body Language of Dating; Simon & Schuster.

LEADERSHIP

- Cabane, Olivia Fox (2012) The Charisma Myth Portfolio; Penguin.

- Goman, Carol Kinsey(2011) The Silent Language of Leadership Jossey-Bass

Smith, Jacquelyn; 10 nonverbal cues that convey confidence at work; 11/3/13 - Forbes eZine.

http://www.forbes.com/sites/jacquelynsmith/2013/03/11/10-nonverbal-cues-that-convey-confidence-at-work/

- Navarro, Joe (2013) Lifehacker - Five mistakes that can ruin any handshake;

http://lifehacker.com/avoid-these-five-mistakes-and-never-give-a-bad-handshak-1178784076

SCHOOL AND GRADES

- The Collegian. - http://hbucollegian.com/?p=8236

CLASSROOM SEATING POSITION AND COLLEGE GRADES

- El Khoury, Amanda (Sept 11, 2012) Daily Sundial: Do better grades depend on seating in class?

http://sundial.csun.edu/2012/09/do-better-grades-depend-on-seating-in-class/

ON LYING, DECEPTION, ETC.

- Leiberman, David J. (1998) Never be lied to again; St. Martin's Press.

- Huston, Philip, Floyd, Michael, Carnicero (2012) Spy the Lie; St. Martin's Press.

- Meyer, Pamela (2011) Ted Talks: How to Spot a Liar.

http://www.youtube.com/watch?v=P_6vDLq64gE

ADDITIONAL BIBLIOGRAPHY

- Mark L Knapp & Judith Hall: Nonverbal Communication in Human Interactions

Cengage Learning – 7th Edition

- David Matsumoto, Mark G Frank, Hyi Sung Huang (Editors) – Nonverbal Communications: Science and Applications

Sage Publications – 1st Edition

- Pete Anderson – Nonverbal Communication: Forms and Functions

Waveland Press – 2nd Edition

- Paul Ekman – Emotions Revealed

Holt Paperbacks – 2nd Edition

- Virginia Peck Richmond, James C. McCroskey Mark L. Hickson – Nonverbal Communication in Interpersonal Relations

Pearson: 7th Edition

- Dale Leathers late, Michael H. Eaves: <u>Successful Nonverbal Principles and Applications</u>

Pearson – 4th Edition

- Paul Ekman: <u>Telling Lies</u>

W.W. Norton: Revised Edition

- Joseph A. DeVito: <u>The Nonverbal Communication Book</u>

Kendall Hunt Publishing – 1st Edition

ENDNOTE

Thanks for buying this book. I think it will help you become a better communicator and learn more about yourself. Studying body language often comes down to just paying attention; watching what other people do, and monitoring your own behavior. Successful interactions require energy, attention, and focus; even more so when maintaining a relationship. One of the most important lessons I can leave you with is: in your busy day-to-day life – it's the people who are most important. Spend the majority of your time and energy on them, and you can't go wrong.

Be well, and pay attention.

WANT MORE?

I offer longer chapters and essays that delve more deeply into many of these topics. You will also find eBook downloads.

Last of all, I'd love to hear from you! Many of the topics in this book were first introduced during the question and answer period of my presentations. Contact me through my website with your question; I'll answer it personally, and I may possibly include it in a later edition of this book!

For speaking inquiries for your school or business, and for updates to this book, please visit my website www.christophercartermentalist.com.